In Other Words

In Other Words

LIFE SKILLS VOCABULARY IN CONTEXT

Teacher's Edition

KATHLEEN A. SANTOPIETRO

Dormac, Inc.

Executive Editor: Carlos Byfield
Editor: Karen Hannabarger
Art Director: Jana C. Whitney
Design: Jill Pittsford
Illustrations: Kim Muslusky
Cover Design: Patti Bergin-Gallup

Dormac, Inc.
P.O. Box 270459
San Diego, California 92128-0983

ISBN 0-86575-651-1
Printed in U.S.A.

Contents

Acknowledgments

Field test sites and coordinators

Barbara Sample
Director of Educational Services
Spring Institute for International Studies
Wheat Ridge, Colorado

Margaret Silver
Director of Education
International Institute
St. Louis, Missouri

Lucy Stromquist
Area Resource Teacher
St. Vrain Valley Schools
Longmont, Colorado

Reviewers and technical assistance

Virginia French Allen
Academic Consultant
Spring Institute for International Studies
Wheat Ridge, Colorado

Dian Bates
State Director
Adult Basic Education
Denver, Colorado

Mark A. Clarke
Associate Professor and Chair
Language, Literacy, and Culture
School of Education
University of Colorado at Denver
Denver, Colorado

The author wishes to thank Ruth and Elvin Graves for their words of support and encouragement.

Inspiration for this book belongs to Leonard and our Saratoga friends.

Introduction

Vocabulary is an important component of language. Because many core ESL texts provide only an introduction to vocabulary, teachers often need supplemental material that focuses on word meaning and usage.

In Other Words: Life Skills Vocabulary in Context provides meaningful activities that reinforce and enhance the vocabulary used in survival English settings. While a core life skills text may provide vocabulary through dialogue, grammar lessons, or pronunciation exercises, students may need further vocabulary practice. The material in this book has been designed to accompany and complement instruction in a life skills curriculum.

The material is suitable for adult learners who have recently arrived in the United States and have had little or no experience in life skills curricula. Many of the activities in each unit can easily be used in multilevel classrooms or in one-to-one tutoring situations. The difficulty level of the exercises does not exceed the intermediate learner's abilities.

Each of the ten units identifies vocabulary of life skills topics that are common in adult ESL classrooms: personal information, health, housing, American government, shopping for food and clothing, transportation, community services, money and banking, and employment.

Each of the ten units contains the following activities. The names of the activities have been chosen to teach students some common expressions in American English.

Picture It

The illustrations at the beginning of each unit provide meaning for life skills vocabulary used in the exercises.

Rather than introducing all vocabulary items before beginning the exercises, the teacher refers to the pictures while students complete the unit. If all the vocabulary is introduced before beginning the unit, students will have difficulty remembering meaning, pronunciation, and usage. The teacher should explain the words in the context of the unit activities.

The pictures in the student's edition are not labeled. Learning meaning before seeing the written word facilitates comprehension and correct pronunciation. After meaning is clear and students can identify vocabulary items, they can label the pictures in their books.

Give It a Try

This oral word substitution exercise provides practice of words in context.

After word meaning is introduced through pictures, the teacher presents each group of phrases orally with students' books closed. When students master the phrases, they can open their books and read the phrases together.

Oral presentation with books closed begins with the teacher modeling the phrase. The students repeat the phrase. Then the teacher gives a cue word. The students repeat the phrase using the new cue word. Here's an example:

Teacher: My leg hurts.

Students: My leg hurts.

Teacher: Arm.

Students: My arm hurts.

Teacher: Head.

Students: My head hurts.

Attention, Please!

This multiple choice exercise provides practice in listening and reading.

Students have three possible responses to each teacher's cue. The teacher's cues are available only in the teacher's edition. The teacher reads each cue twice in normal speech. The students listen, then circle the correct response. After students complete the exercise, the teacher checks the students' responses orally.

Tell Me About It

In this pair activity, one student has information that another student needs, but doesn't have, to complete a task.

The teacher divides the class into pairs. One student in each pair uses Part A; the other uses Part B. Parts A and B are back-to-back pages in the student's edition. Partners are seated so that they can't see each other's pages. Partners take turns asking questions about items shown on the other student's page. Using directional words and other clues, each student provides his or her partner with locations, costs, and other information not shown on the partner's page. The partner then writes the new information in the appropriate place on the page. The teacher monitors the activity by listening to each pair. After students have finished labeling their pages, they check their communication by looking at both Part A and Part B.

Guess Who, Where, or What

This category exercise checks students' understanding of word meanings.

This activity can be used in multilevel classes. The teacher divides the class into pairs of students. Each pair reads the list of words and phrases and decides which category each word or phrase belongs to. Then the students write the word or phrase in the correct category.

This activity can also be completed by individual students if the pair activity does not facilitate learning.

Two Against One

This category exercise makes use of reading and speaking skills and checks students' understanding of word meaning and usage.

Students complete the page by reading the three words in each set and then circling the word that doesn't belong to the set. After students have finished the exercise, the teacher checks the students' answers orally, asking individuals to explain their choices. In some exercise items, more than one answer is acceptable. The students' explanation of their choices determines acceptable answers.

Inside Story

This fill in the blank exercise facilitates students' use of contextual clues, provides practice in finding synonyms, and fosters the skill of analysis.

The students first read the story. Then they find words from the word list that have the same meanings as the words under the blank lines in the story. Students write the matching words on the blanks. When all the blanks are filled, students read the story using the new terms.

Take Your Pick

This is a multiple choice exercise that checks students' understanding of vocabulary usage in sentences.

Students choose the words or phrases missing in each sentence from among the three choices listed under the sentence. Prefixes and suffixes that change word meaning appear in some of the answer choices. Students write the missing word or phrase on the blank in the sentence.

Bingo

Students create their own bingo cards through teacher dictation of vocabulary. The dictation provides a spelling assessment as well as a listening activity.

Before beginning the bingo game, the teacher may need to explain the rules of bingo for the benefit of students who have never played before.

Each unit contains two game options for bingo. The teacher either chooses the option that best fits the students' level of proficiency or uses the two options at different times of instruction.

Get It Together

This crossword puzzle provides practice in recognizing word meaning and usage.

A list of the crossword puzzle vocabulary is given in addition to the numbered puzzle clues so that spelling will not hinder students' ability to complete the puzzle. The teacher can quiz the spelling skills of more advanced students by asking them to cover the word list while filling in the puzzle squares.

And There's More

This section of additional games and activities appears only in the teacher's edition. It contains suggestions for classroom activities and small group discussions.

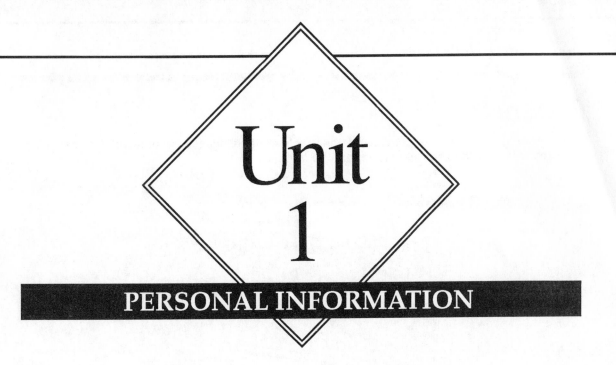

Unit 1

PERSONAL INFORMATION

Picture It

The following pictures provide meaning for the life skills vocabulary used throughout the unit.

In this unit, the pictures illustrate the concepts of marital status and employment status. Pictures also show the American forms for expressing name, address, birth date, and other important numbers. In addition, they provide examples of important identification documents, including a Social Security card and a driver's license. Physical characteristics important for identification purposes are also shown.

Rather than introducing all vocabulary items before beginning the exercises, refer to the pictures while students complete the unit. If all the vocabulary is introduced before beginning the unit, students will have difficulty remembering meaning, pronunciation, and usage. Introduce the words in the context of the unit activities. For example, before asking students to complete "Guess Who, Where, or What," use the pictures to show word meanings for the vocabulary in that exercise.

Pictures in the student's edition are not labeled. Learning meaning before seeing the written word facilitates comprehension and correct pronunciation. When introducing the vocabulary in the pictures, you may want to model each word and have the class repeat it after you. Give examples of the word in sentences. After meaning is clear and students can identify vocabulary items, they can label the pictures with your assistance. Once students have labeled the pictures, they can use this section to review word meaning and spelling.

Picture It

The following pictures show people and things that will be discussed in this unit. Refer to these pictures when doing exercises throughout the unit.

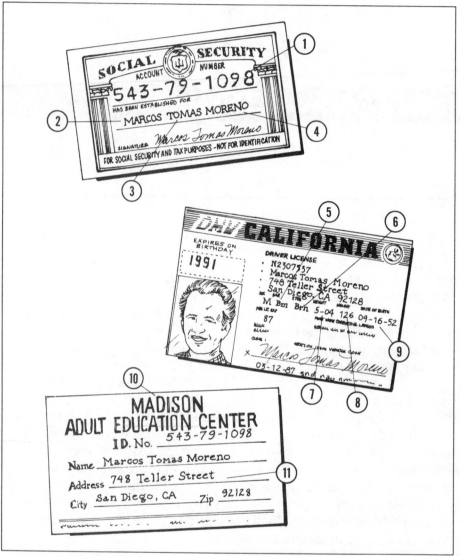

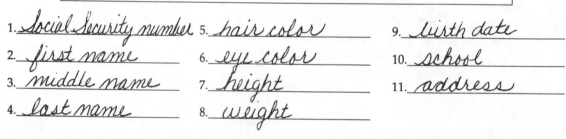

1. _Social Security number_   5. _hair color_   9. _birth date_
2. _first name_   6. _eye color_   10. _school_
3. _middle name_   7. _height_   11. _address_
4. _last name_   8. _weight_

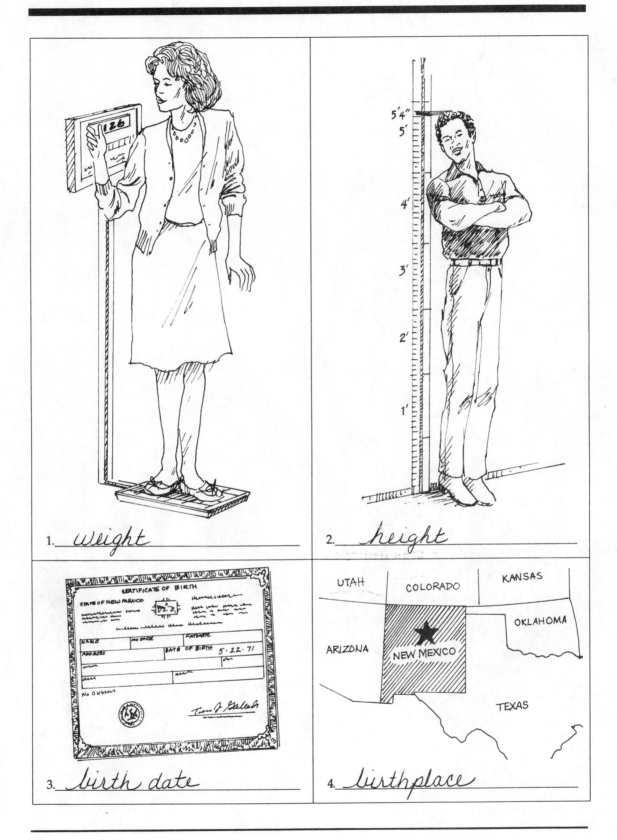

1. *weight*

2. *height*

3. *birth date*

4. *birthplace*

5. *male and female*

6. *single*

7. *married*

8. *separated*

9. *divorced*

10. *widowed*

11. *employed*

12. *unemployed*

MARCOS TOMAS MORENO

13. first name

MARCOS TOMAS MORENO

14. last name

MARCOS TOMAS MORENO

15. middle name

16. eye color

17. hair color

18. signature

Marcos Tomas Moreno

(619) 694-7311

19. phone number

Marcos T. Moreno
748 Teller Street
San Diego, Ca 92128

20. address

Give It a Try

This exercise provides practice of words in context.

After word meaning is introduced through pictures, read each group of phrases orally with the students' books closed. After the students master the phrases, they can open their books and read the phrases together.

You may need to explain words unfamiliar to the students before beginning the exercise. Begin the oral presentation by modeling each phrase. Have the students repeat the phrase. Then give a cue word. The students repeat the sentence with the new cue word.

Give It a Try

Practice the phrases listed below.

1. Write your __last name__ here.
   first name
   middle name
   height

2. What's your __birth date__? __May 15, 1969__
   birthplace   San Salvador
   ZIP Code   90056
   area code   213

3. What __city__ does he live in? __Austin__
   apartment   number 308
   state   Texas

4. She lives alone, she is __single__.
   divorced
   separated
   widowed

5. He has been __married__ for eight years.
   divorced
   employed
   unemployed

6. What's your __work__ address? __1986 Fell Street__
   home   1355 56th Street
   school   1219 Grand Avenue

7. Write your __telephone__ number here.
   Social Security
   work
   apartment

8. __Marcos__ circled __male__ on the application.
   Marta   female
   Ray   Mr.
   Tury   Mrs.

Example:

Teacher: What's your birth date?

Students: What's your birth date?

Teacher: ZIP Code.

Students: What's your ZIP Code?

Teacher: Area code.

Students: What's your area code?

Attention, Please!

This exercise provides practice in listening and reading.

Read each oral cue twice in normal speech. The cues are available only in the teacher's edition. Students listen to the cue, read the three choices in their books, and then circle the word or phrase identified by the cue. After the students complete the exercise, check their responses orally.

Attention, Please!

Listen to the teacher's cue. Then, circle the correct response.

1. birth date — (birthplace) — city
2. ZIP Code — area code — (address)
3. apartment — (phone number) — address
4. (birth date) — birthplace — height
5. (height) — ZIP Code — weight
6. (Social Security number) — mailing address — home address
7. married — single — (widowed)
8. first name — (last name) — middle name
9. height — (weight) — married
10. ZIP Code — phone number — (area code)
11. (145 pounds) — 5' 7" — 89076
12. (9/4/50) — 135 pounds — 432-0987

Teacher Cues

1. Born in Mexico.
2. Eighty-nine seventy-six Smith Street.
3. Five four three [pause] eight seven six five.
4. Born on seven nine sixty-two.
5. Five feet, six inches.
6. Three seven oh [pause] nine eight [pause] oh oh seven eight.
7. His wife died.
8. Family name.
9. One hundred and fifty pounds.
10. Three oh three.
11. Weight.
12. Birth date.

Tell Me About It

This is a pair activity. One student has information that another student needs, but doesn't have, in order to complete a task.

Divide the class into pairs of students. One person in each pair uses Part A; the other uses Part B. Parts A and B are back-to-back pages in the student's edition. Partners should be seated so that they can't see each other's pages. Partners take turns asking questions about items in the pictures. Referring to the visual clues and using directional words, students answer each other's questions and write the new information in the correct places on the pictures.

Monitor the activity by listening to each pair of students. After students complete all the questions, ask them to check their communication by comparing Parts A and B.

Tell Me About It (Part A)

Study the application form. Then, ask your partner the questions below. Fill in the form with your partner's answers.

What's the person's last name?
What's his street address?
What's his phone number?
What's his birth date?
How tall is he?

How old is he?
What's the date?
What state does he live in?
What city does he live in?

Name *Lopez* *Sam* *Luis*
LAST   FIRST   MIDDLE

Address *526 Blue Street*   *#42*
STREET   APT. NO.

Denver   *Colorado*   *80221*
CITY   STATE   ZIP CODE

Telephone Number (*303*) *778- 4120*
AREA CODE

Height *5'7"*   Weight *145 lbs.*   Age *36*

Birth Date *6/15/52*   Birthplace *México*
DAY / MO. / YR.

[ ] Married [X] Single [ ] Divorced [ ] Separated [ ] Widowed

[X] Employed [ ] Unemployed

Place of Employment *Smith Machine Shop*

Signature *Sam L. Lopez*   Date *April 4, 1989*

Tell Me About It (Part B)

Study the application form. Then, ask your partner the questions below. Fill in the form with your partner's answers.

What's the person's first name?   How much does he weigh?
What's his middle name?   Is he married?
What's the apartment number?   Where was he born?
What's the area code?   Where is he working?
What's the ZIP Code?

Name __Lopez_____ _____Sam_____ ____Luis____
              LAST   FIRST   MIDDLE

Address __526 Blue Street_____ ___#42___
                    STREET   APT. NO.

__Denver_____ __Colorado_____ __80221__
     CITY   STATE   ZIP CODE

Telephone Number (_303_) _778-4120_____
                        AREA CODE

Height _5'7"_____ Weight _145 lbs.__ Age _36__

Birth Date __6/15/52_____ Birthplace __Mexico_____
                 DAY / MO. / YR.

[ ] Married [X] Single [ ] Divorced [ ] Separated [ ] Widowed

[X] Employed [ ] Unemployed

Place of Employment __Smith Machine Shop_____

Signature __Sam L. Lopez_____ Date __April 4, 1989__

Guess Who, Where, or What

This is a category exercise that can be used with pairs of students in multilevel classes. It can also be completed by individual students. Having students list words under appropriate categories checks their understanding of word meanings.

Students read each word or phrase in the list and decide if it describes a person, place, or thing. Then each student writes the word or phrase in the correct category. You should categorize the first word to provide an example for the students.

Guess Who, Where, or What

Read each word or phrase in the list below. Ask a classmate if the word or phrase describes a person, place, or thing. Write the words in the correct category.

married	single	ZIP Code
address	area code	phone number
Social Security number	divorced	weight
widowed	age	middle name
first name	state	city
birth date	birthplace	height
last name	male	female
employed	unemployed	place of employment

Words That Describe Us	Information Places	Information Numbers
married	address	Social Security number
widowed	state	birth date
first name	birthplace	area code
last name	city	age
employed	place of employment	Zip Code
single		phone number
divorced		weight
male		height
unemployed		
middle name		
female		

Two Against One

This category exercise checks students' understanding of word meaning and usage. Explain the concept of a set to the class before beginning the exercise.

Ask students to read the three words in each set and then circle the word that doesn't belong to the set. Check the exercise orally by asking students to explain their choices. More than one answer is acceptable in some exercise sets. The students' explanation of their choices determines acceptable answers.

Two Against One

Circle the word that doesn't belong to the set. Explain your choice to the class.

1. first name   last name   (address)

2. divorced   (married)   separated

3. (ZIP Code)   area code   phone number

4. city   (female)   state

5. (state)   male   female

6. employed   (unemployed)   place of employment

7. (married)   single   divorced

8. height   weight   (face)

9. last name   (ZIP Code)   signature

10. age   (birthplace)   birth date

11. 120 pounds   weight   (height)

12. height   5'8"   (ZIP Code)

Inside Story

This activity facilitates students' use of contextual clues and provides practice in finding synonyms. Rather than just measuring basic comprehension of vocabulary, the exercise fosters the skill of analysis.

First ask the students to read the entire story. Then ask them to find words from the word list that have the same meanings as the words under the blank lines in the story. Instruct the students to write the matching words on the blanks. You may want to fill in the first blank to provide the students with an example. When all the matching words are found and all the blanks are filled in, students should read the story again using the new words.

Inside Story

Read the story below. Choose words or phrases from the list that have the same meanings as the words or phrases under the lines. Write the correct words on the blanks. Read the story again using the words written on the blanks.

middle name	picture	glad
renew	weight	height
identification	address	city
last name	answer	test
age	birth date	

Juanita's Driver's License

Juanita went to _renew_ (replace) her driver's license. She passed the written _test_ (exam). She passed the driving test. Then, she had to _answer_ (respond to) some questions.

The clerk asked for the spelling of her _last name_ (family name). Juanita spelled her _middle name_ (second name) too. She gave her new _address_ (house number). She lives in the same _city_ (town) but moved to a new apartment last month.

The officer asked Juanita for her _height_ (how tall she is) and _weight_ (how much she weighs) and her eye and hair color. He also needed to know her _birth date_ (day of birth) and _age_ (how old she is). After the questions, the officer took Juanita's _picture_ (photo) for _identification_ (I.D.). Juanita smiled. She was _glad_ (happy) it was over.

Take Your Pick

This multiple choice exercise measures students' understanding of vocabulary meaning and usage in sentences.

Review the unit vocabulary using the pictures at the beginning of the unit. Explain any other new vocabulary in the exercise items before asking students to complete the exercise.

Tell the students to choose the word or phrase missing in each sentence from among the three choices listed under the sentence. Prefixes and suffixes that change word meaning appear in some of the answer choices. Have students write the missing word or phrase on the blank in each sentence.

Take Your Pick

There is a missing word or phrase in each sentence below. Read each sentence. Then, look at the three choices under the sentence. Choose the correct word or phrase and write it on the blank.

1. He circled the word _male_ on his application form.

   female   male   sex

2. Fidel lives in the _state_ of California.

   area code   address   state

3. Tom's _birth date_ is May 26, 1948.

   birthplace   birth date   city

4. Lupe gave her _height_ as 5 feet, 2 inches.

   height   weight   hair color

5. Write your _last name_ first.

   name last   first   last name

6. Binh gave his _weight_ as 135 pounds

   weight   height   phone number

7. What's your _Social Security number_ ?

   Social number Security   Social Security number   Security Social number

8. _Sign_ at the bottom, please.

   Signs   Signing   Sign

9. Maria has been _married_ for 12 years.

   married   marriage   marry

10. Write the _area code_ before the phone number.

    ZIP Code   city   area code

Bingo

1. Make the bingo cards.

Students create bingo cards through teacher dictation of vocabulary. The dictation provides a spelling assessment as well as a listening activity.

Instruct the students to look at the empty bingo grid in their book. The grid has nine squares for nine vocabulary items. Read the vocabulary to the class. Ask students to write the words in the boxes at random, not in rows. Each student should have a different bingo card after nine items are dictated.

2. Check students' spelling.

When the bingo cards are completed, write the vocabulary words on the board and ask students to check their spelling and make corrections.

3. Play bingo.

Distribute eight markers — such as paper clips, buttons, chips, or pennies — to each student. Read each oral cue twice in normal speech. Students find the corresponding vocabulary item on their cards and cover it with a marker. When one student has three in a row, he or she calls "bingo" and then reads off the words in the marked squares for checking. You may need to demonstrate how bingo is played for those students who have never played before.

There are two game options. Choose the one that best fits the students' level of proficiency, or use them both at different times of instruction.

Game 1

Vocabulary for Dictation	Teacher Cues
birth date	October twenty-first [pause] nineteen seventy-five.
birthplace	Home country.
phone number	Six five seven [pause] oh nine eight seven.
ZIP Code	Eight oh two nine seven.
area code	Three oh three.
male	Man.
female	Woman.
height	Six feet three inches.
weight	One hundred and sixty-five pounds.

Game 2

Vocabulary for Dictation	Teacher Cues
employed	Having a job.
unemployed	Not having a job.
Social Security number	Six five four [pause] nine oh [pause] eight seven six five.
divorced	Husband and wife are apart.
widowed	Husband or wife is not living.
date	[Give today's date.]
place of employment	Where you work
last name	Family name.
address	One ninety-eight James Street.

Get It Together

The crossword puzzle provides practice in recognizing word meaning and usage.

Have students read each numbered clue and write the answer in the puzzle spaces with the same number. A word list of answers is given so that spelling will not hinder students' ability to complete the puzzle.

To quiz the spelling skills of more advanced students, ask the students to cover the word list while filling in the puzzle squares.

Get It Together

There is a word missing in each sentence below. Choose the correct word from the word list. Print that word in the boxes of the puzzle.

city	Code	height
information	name	first
married	single	birth
address	age	Social

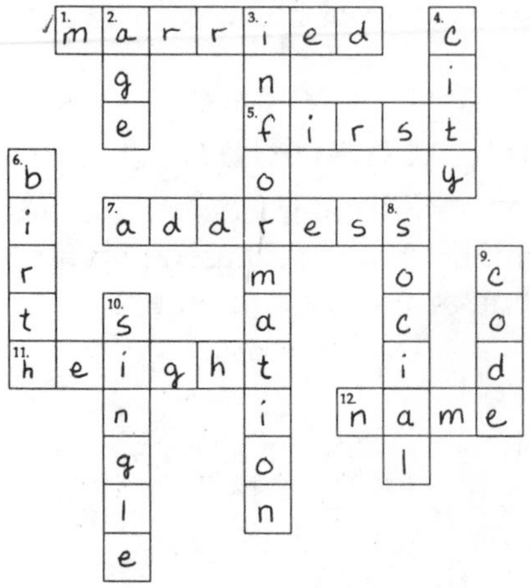

Across

1. She was ________ to Emilio for 12 years.
5. Her ________ name is Mary.
7. His ________ is 509 Reed Place.
11. His ________ is 6'2".
12. What's your last ________ ?

Down

2. She gave her ________ as 45 years.
3. They ask for personal ________ .
4. Every ________ has a different ZIP Code.
6. His ________ date is 4/12/52.
8. What's your ________ Security number?
9. What's your ZIP ________ ?
10. She's not married; she's ________ .

16 ◆ Unit 1

And There's More

1. Yellow Pages

In this activity the class creates a *Yellow Pages Classroom Directory*. Give each student a sheet of yellow paper. Ask the students to write personal information about themselves on the yellow paper. The information may be given in a list or in composition form.

Ask for the following information:

address	eye color
phone number	hair color
Social Security number	weight
birthplace	height
employment information	birth date

You may want to add two other categories of personal information to the list, skills and hobbies. Since these two words were not introduced in this unit, you may need to explain their meanings and give examples.

When students have completed their pages, ask them to put the pages in alphabetical order according to last names. The class can create a cover for the pages, then staple the pages together.

2. Guess Who?

Begin this guessing activity by giving a description of a student in the classroom without mentioning his or her name. Here's an example:

> "I'm thinking of a person who has brown hair and green eyes. This person is about 35 years old and was born in Mexico. This person is female. She works at the bakery at the supermarket."

Students try to guess which classmate is being described after each sentence of the description is given. You may have to give more specific clues as the description continues. Those clues could be where the person is sitting in the room or a description of his or her clothing.

After you have demonstrated the guessing game, students can take turns giving descriptions of each other. You may need to remind students not to look at the person they are describing.

3. Role Play

Divide the class into pairs of students. You may want to consider student literacy and oral proficiency levels in assigning pairs, putting more skilled students with those at lower levels of ability.

Assign each pair a situation from the list below. Students may want to choose the situation they prefer.

- a job interview
- admittance to a hospital
- application for a loan
- registration at school
- application for a driver's license

The first pair task is to design an application form. Ask the pairs to make a list of the kind of information that is needed in the situation. Then ask the pairs to create the application forms using the list of information. You may need to circulate among the students to answer questions or give advice.

After the forms have been created, the students role play. One person in the pair plays an interviewer; the other, the person being interviewed. The interviewer asks the questions and records the responses of the other person until the form is completed.

Unit 2

HEALTH

Picture It

The following pictures provide meaning for the life skills vocabulary used throughout the unit.

The pictures in this unit familiarize students with health-care professionals and facilities enabling students to feel comfortable securing medical assistance. Identified body parts and common ailments help students to describe symptoms to a doctor. Medical instruments and types of medication are also shown.

Rather than introducing all vocabulary items before beginning the exercises, refer to the pictures while students complete the unit. If all the vocabulary is introduced before beginning the unit, students will have difficulty remembering meaning, pronunciation, and usage. Introduce the words in the context of the unit activities. For example, before asking students to complete "Guess Who, Where, or What," use the pictures to show word meanings for the vocabulary in that exercise.

Pictures in the student's edition are not labeled. Learning meaning before seeing the written word facilitates comprehension and correct pronunciation. When introducing the vocabulary in the pictures, you may want to model each word and have the class repeat it after you. Give examples of the word in sentences. After meaning is clear and students can identify vocabulary items, they can label the pictures with your assistance. Once students have labeled the pictures, they can use this section to review word meaning and spelling.

Picture It

The following pictures show people and things that will be discussed in this unit. Refer to these pictures when doing exercises throughout the unit.

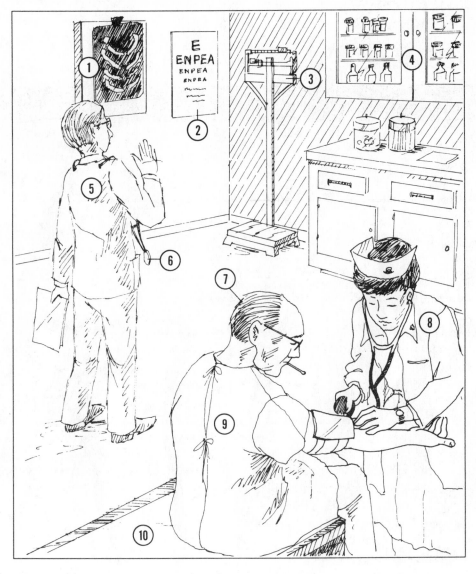

1. _X-ray_
2. _eye chart_
3. _scale_
4. _medicine cabinet_
5. _doctor_
6. _stethoscope_
7. _patient_
8. _nurse_
9. _gown_
10. _examining table_

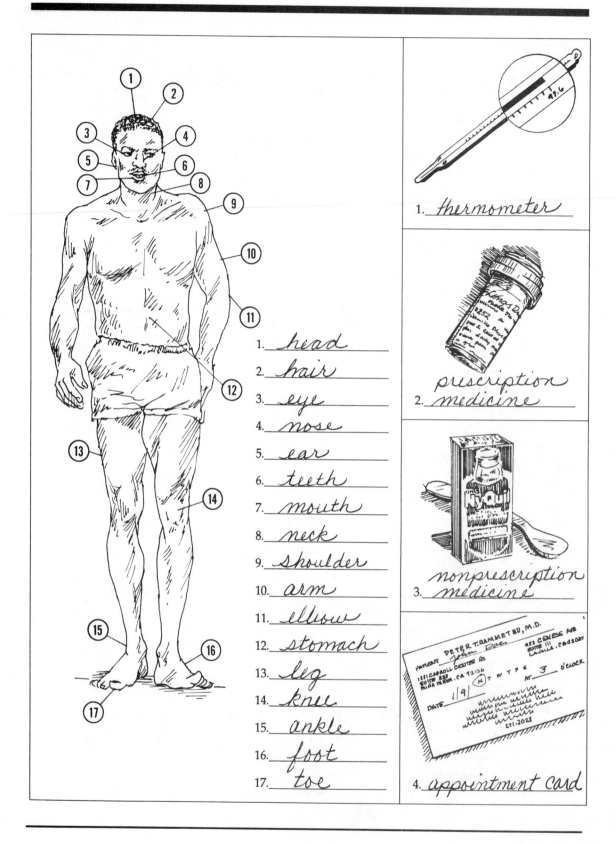

1. thermometer

prescription
2. medicine

nonprescription
3. medicine

4. appointment card

1. head
2. hair
3. eye
4. nose
5. ear
6. teeth
7. mouth
8. neck
9. shoulder
10. arm
11. elbow
12. stomach
13. leg
14. knee
15. ankle
16. foot
17. toe

5. *surgeon*

6. *therapist*

7. *ambulance driver*

8. *pharmacist*

9. *receptionist*

10. *nurse*

11. _sore throat_

12. _headache_

13. _backache_

14. _stomachache_

15. _toothache_

16. _earache_

17. _cough_

18. _fever_

19. _broken arm_

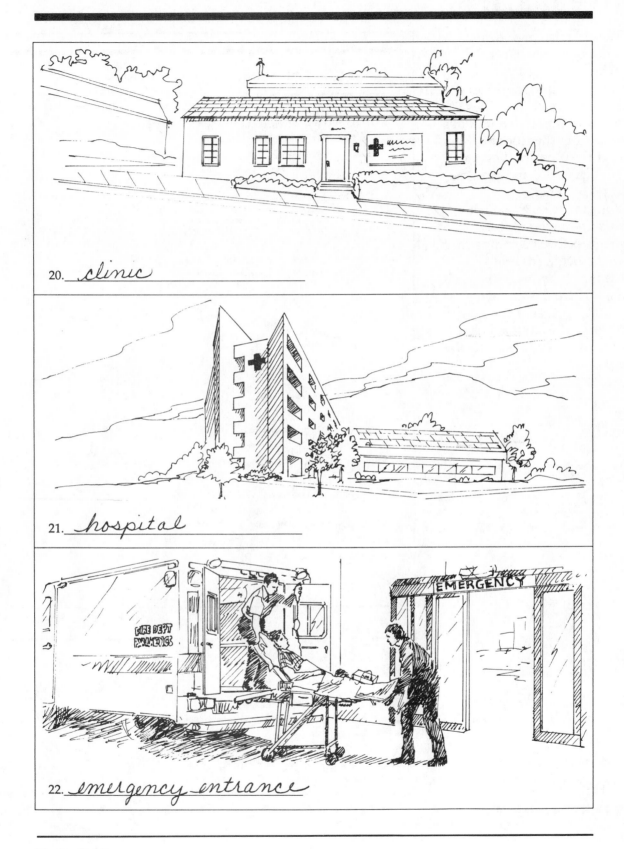

20. *clinic*

21. *hospital*

22. *emergency entrance*

Give It a Try

This exercise provides practice of words in context.

After word meaning is introduced through pictures, read each group of phrases orally with the students' books closed. After the students master the phrases, they can open their books and read the phrases together.

You may need to explain words unfamiliar to the students before beginning the exercise. Begin the oral presentation by <u>modeling</u> each phrase. Have the students repeat the phrase. Then give a <u>cue</u> word. The <u>students repeat</u> the sentence with the new cue word.

Give It a Try

Practice the phrases listed below.

1. Did they check your <u>blood pressure</u> at the clinic? <u>Yes, they did</u>.

        temperature
        pulse
        heartbeat   No, they didn't
        X-rays

2. My son has a <u>headache</u>. He should <u>buy some aspirin</u>.

      backache   get some rest
      toothache   see the dentist
      sore throat   see the doctor

3. Where is the <u>hospital</u>? It's <u>across the street</u>.

      clinic   two blocks away
      pharmacy   straight down the hall
      emergency room   on the first floor

4. My <u>chest</u> hurts. My <u>shoulders</u> hurt.

      leg   feet
      arm   eyes
      ankle   fingers
      foot   hands

5. The <u>doctor</u> is at the <u>clinic</u>.

      surgeon   hospital
      therapist   office
      pharmacist   drugstore

6. You may buy <u>some aspirin</u> at the drugstore.

        some cough syrup
        a thermometer
        some medicine

7. The <u>doctor</u> uses a <u>stethoscope</u> in an exam.

      nurse   thermometer
              blood pressure cuff
              scale

Example:

Teacher: My chest hurts.

Students: My chest hurts.

Teacher: Leg.

Students: My leg hurts.

Teacher: Ankle.

Students: My ankle hurts.

Attention, Please!

This exercise provides practice in listening and reading.

Explain words unfamiliar to the students before beginning the exercise.

Read each oral cue twice in normal speech. The cues are available only in the teacher's edition. Students listen to the cue, read the three choices in their books, and then circle the word or phrase identified by the cue. After the students complete the exercise, check their responses orally.

Attention, Please!

Listen to the teacher's cue. Then, circle the correct response.

1.	patient	(surgeon)	pharmacist
2.	(patient)	surgeon	therapist
3.	nurse	doctor	(pharmacist)
4.	nurse	(doctor)	pharmacist
5.	(therapist)	ambulance driver	receptionist
6.	nurse	(receptionist)	patient
7.	blood pressure cuff	(thermometer)	stethoscope
8.	(stethoscope)	blood sample	thermometer
9.	prescription medicine	(nonprescription medicine)	pharmacy
10.	eye chart	surgeon	(scale)
11.	broken arm	shoulders	(fever)
12.	clinic	(hospital)	X-ray lab

Teacher Cues

1. She operates.
2. He is sick.
3. She prepares medicine.
4. He writes a prescription.
5. He teaches exercises.
6. She makes appointments.
7. It tells temperature.
8. The doctor uses this to listen to your heart.
9. Aspirin and cough syrup.
10. It tells your height or weight.
11. A high temperature.
12. It has an emergency entrance.

Tell Me About It

This is a pair activity. One student has information that another student needs, but doesn't have, in order to complete a task.

Before asking students to complete this exercise, you may want to review prepositions of location (*on, under, behind, next to, in, above,* etc.) and directional words (*left, right, straight, up,* and *down*).

Divide the class into pairs of students. One person in each pair uses Part A; the other uses Part B. Parts A and B are back-to-back pages in the student's edition. Partners should be seated so that they can't see each other's pages. Partners take turns asking questions about items in the pictures. Referring to the visual clues and using directional words, students answer each other's questions and write the new information in the correct places on the pictures.

Monitor the activity by listening to each pair of students. After students complete all the questions, ask them to check their communication by comparing Parts A and B.

Tell Me About It (Part A)

Study the picture. Then, ask your partner the questions below. Using your partner's answers, write the name of each underlined item in the correct place on the picture.

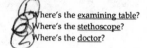

Where's the <u>examining table</u>?
Where's the <u>stethoscope</u>?
Where's the <u>doctor</u>?

Where's the <u>thermometer</u>?
Where's the <u>scale</u>?
Where's the <u>gown</u>?

Tell Me About It (Part B)

Study the picture. Then, ask your partner the questions below. Using your partner's answers, write the name of each underlined item in the correct place on the picture.

Where's the <u>X-ray</u>?   Where's the <u>blood pressure cuff</u>?
Where's the <u>medicine cabinet</u>?   Where's the <u>eye chart</u>?
Where's the <u>blood sample</u>?   Where's the <u>nurse</u>?

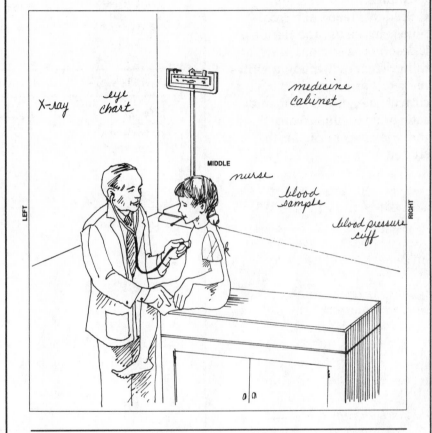

Guess Who, Where, or What

This is a category exercise that can be used with pairs of students in multilevel classes. It can also be completed by individual students. Having students list words under appropriate categories checks their understanding of word meanings.

Students read each word or phrase in the list and decide if it describes a person, place, or thing. Then each student writes the word or phrase in the correct category. You should categorize the first word to provide an example for the students.

Guess Who, Where, or What

Read each word or phrase in the list below. Ask a classmate if the word or phrase describes a person, place, or thing. Write the words in the correct category.

doctor
blood pressure cuff
hospital
gown
ambulance driver
pharmacist
examining room
emergency room

nurse
clinic
eye chart
blood sample
surgeon
stethoscope
receptionist

therapist
thermometer
examining table
X-ray lab
pharmacy
X-ray
scale

Health Workers	Places for Health Services	Things a Doctor Uses
doctor	hospital	blood pressure cuff
ambulance driver	examining room	gown
pharmacist	emergency room	eye chart
nurse	clinic	blood sample
surgeon	X-ray lab	stethoscope
receptionist	pharmacy	thermometer
therapist		examining table
		X-ray
		scale

Two Against One

This category exercise checks students' understanding of word meaning and usage.

Explain the concept of a set to the class before beginning the exercise.

Ask students to read the three words in each set and then circle the word that doesn't belong to the set. Check the exercise orally by asking students to explain their choices. More than one answer is acceptable in some exercise sets. The students' explanation of their choices determines acceptable answers.

Two Against One

Circle the word that doesn't belong to the set. Explain your choice to the class.

1.	headache	(back)	backache
2.	nose	mouth	(shoulder)
3.	emergency	hospital	(pharmacy)
4.	(ankle)	waist	stomach
5.	pain	(hospital)	ache
6.	feet	ankle	(arm)
7.	temperature	(nurse)	thermometer
8.	(patient)	doctor	nurse
9.	(face)	eyes	ears
10.	appointment	(emergency)	clinic
11.	stethoscope	(X-ray lab)	thermometer
12.	(prescription)	aspirin	nonprescription

Inside Story

This activity facilitates students' use of contextual clues and provides practice in finding synonyms. Rather than just measuring basic comprehension of vocabulary, the exercise fosters the skill of analysis.

First ask the students to read the entire story. Then ask them to find words from the word list that have the same meanings as the words under the blank lines in the story. Instruct the students to write the matching words on the blanks. You may want to fill in the first blank to provide the students with an example. When all the matching words are found and all the blanks are filled in, students should read the story again using the new words.

Inside Story

Read the story below. Choose words or phrases from the list that have the same meanings as the words or phrases under the lines. Write the correct words on the blanks. Read the story again using the words written on the blanks.

doctor	clinic	sick
8	got up	thermometer
3:00 P.M.	fever	receptionist
sore throat	stay in bed	100°
headache	an appointment	temperature

Manuel Is Sick

Manuel is _____ *8* _____ years old. Today he
(eight)

_____ *got up* _____ late. He was _____ *sick* _____ . He had a
(got out of bed)   (not well)

_____ *sore throat* _____ . He had a _____ *headache* _____ . He had a cough.
(pain in his throat)   (pain in his head)

His mother, Juanita, told him to _____ *stay in bed* _____ . Juanita got the
(not get up)

_____ *thermometer* _____ to take her son's _____ *temperature* _____ . It was over
(thing that tells temperature)   (measure of heat)

_____ *100°* _____ ! Manuel had a _____ *fever* _____ .
(one hundred degrees)   (high temperature)

Juanita called the _____ *clinic* _____ to make _____ *an appointment* _____
(place for health care)   (a visit time)

for Manuel. The _____ *receptionist* _____ said Manuel could see the
(person answering)

_____ *doctor* _____ at _____ *3:00 p.m.* _____ .
(Dr.)   (three o'clock in the afternoon)

Take Your Pick

This multiple choice exercise measures students' understanding of vocabulary meaning and usage in sentences.

Review the unit vocabulary using the pictures at the beginning of the unit. Explain any other new vocabulary in the exercise items before asking students to complete the exercise.

Tell the students to choose the word or phrase missing in each sentence from among the three choices listed under the sentence. Prefixes and suffixes that change word meaning appear in some of the answer choices. Have students write the missing word or phrase on the blank in each sentence.

Take Your Pick

There is a missing word or phrase in each sentence below. Read each sentence. Then, look at the three choices under the sentence. Choose the correct word or phrase and write it on the blank.

1. The nurse took his _temperature_ .

    temperature   thermometer   fever

2. Maria called the clinic to make an early _appointment_ .

    appointment   check-up   examination

3. Tuyet needed a _check-up_ for her new job.

    check-out   checkup   check-around

4. Her _prescription_ was filled at the Baker Pharmacy on 7th Street.

    medicine   appointment   prescription

5. Take a deep _breath_ .

    breathe   breath   breathing

6. The boy has a _broken_ leg.

    broken   break   broke

7. Juanita took _aspirin_ for her headache.

    aspirin   surgery   checkup

8. Kim has to have _surgery_ on Tuesday morning.

    surgeon   broken arm   surgery

9. The _pharmacist_ gave me the medicine.

    pharmacist   pharmacy   prescription

10. The nurse took his _blood pressure_ .

    blood press   pressure blood   blood pressure

Bingo

1. Make the bingo cards.

Students create bingo cards through teacher dictation of vocabulary. The dictation provides a spelling assessment as well as a listening activity.

Instruct the students to look at the empty bingo grid in their book. The grid has nine squares for nine vocabulary items. Read the vocabulary to the class. Ask students to write the words in the boxes at random, not in rows. Each student should have a different bingo card after nine items are dictated.

2. Check students' spelling.

When the bingo cards are completed, write the vocabulary words on the board and ask students to check their spelling and make corrections.

3. Play bingo.

Distribute eight markers — such as paper clips, buttons, chips, or pennies — to each student. Read each oral cue twice in normal speech. Students find the corresponding vocabulary item on their cards and cover it with a marker. When one student has three in a row, he or she calls "bingo" and then reads off the words in the marked squares for checking. You may need to demonstrate how bingo is played for those students who have never played before.

There are two game options. Choose the one that best fits the students' level of proficiency, or use them both at different times of instruction.

Game 1

Vocabulary for Dictation	Teacher Cues
fever	A high temperature.
thermometer	It measures temperature.
ambulance	It takes you to a hospital in an emergency.
clinic	Go here for a doctor's appointment.
pharmacy	Go here to have a prescription filled.
X-ray	A picture of your bones.
doctor	A physician.
aspirin	Nonprescription medicine.
patient	A sick person.

Game 2

Vocabulary for Dictation	Teacher Cues
doctor	Take a deep breath, please.
pharmacist	Here's your prescription medicine.
nurse	I'll take a blood sample for the doctor.
ambulance driver	I can get you to the hospital in ten minutes.
surgeon	I will operate on your arm tomorrow.
therapist	Come to therapy at five o'clock tomorrow.
receptionist	Here's your appointment card.
patient	I have a bad headache, doctor.
fever	One hundred and one degrees.

Get It Together

The crossword puzzle provides practice in recognizing word meaning and usage.

Have students read each numbered clue and write the answer in the puzzle spaces with the same number. A word list of answers is given so that spelling will not hinder students' ability to complete the puzzle.

To quiz the spelling skills of more advanced students, ask the students to cover the word list while filling in the puzzle squares.

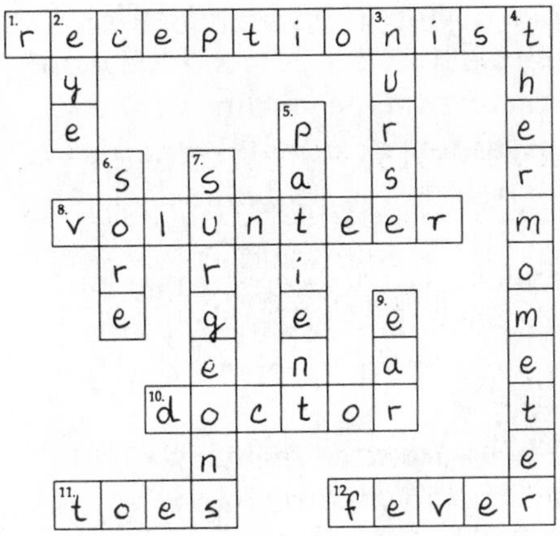

Get It Together

There is a word missing in each sentence below. Choose the correct word from the word list. Print that word in the boxes of the puzzle.

doctor	surgeons	eye
receptionist	fever	thermometer
patient	volunteer	nurse
toes	sore	ear

Across

1. The ________ sits at the information desk.
8. A ________ isn't paid.
10. A physician is a ________.
11. There are ten ________ on two feet.
12. 101° is a ________.

Down

2. He closed his left ________.
3. The ________ took his blood pressure.
4. Use a ________ to take your temperature.
5. The ________ is very sick.
6. I have a ________ throat.
7. Two ________ operated on him.
9. He has wax in his ________.

32 ◆ Unit 2

And There's More

1. Concentration

Copy and cut out individual pictures from the beginning of the unit. Mount the pictures on 3" x 5" cards. Label the back of the pictures with consecutive numbers. On an equal number of cards, write the names of the pictures. Then label the back of the cards with consecutive letters.

Lay all the cards on a large table, pictures and words facing down. Ask students to take turns choosing two cards, trying to match a picture with its word. Ask each student to read the word and identify the picture on the card he or she chooses. Then the student decides if the cards are a match. Check to be sure the student's decision is correct.

If there is no match, the cards are turned back over. If there is a match, the student keeps the pair of cards. The winner is the person who has the most matched cards.

Concentration helps exercise memory, gives review of letter and number names, and reinforces vocabulary.

2. Memory Circle

Have students sit in a circle and ask each to name a part of the body that hurts. You should start the dialogue by naming an item. The first student repeats the item you have named and adds another item. As the game continues, each student repeats what has been said, then adds a body part of his or her choice. Items may or may not be given in alphabetical order. Here's an example of how the activity should progress:

Teacher:	I have to see a doctor. My arm hurts.
First student:	I have to see a doctor. My arm hurts, my back hurts.
Second student:	I have to see a doctor. My arm hurts, my back hurts, my chest hurts.

In multilevel classes beginners should start the process and more advanced students should follow, so that the advanced students have to remember more items.

3. The Man on the Moon

Tell students that you can describe people who live on the moon. Ask students to use their imaginations to draw what you describe. The pictures can be strange and funny. A description can be as follows:

- He has three eyes.
- He has four feet on the top of his head.
- He has long hair.
- He has four hands with six fingers on each.

This activity also can be done in pairs. Students take turns describing the moon people and drawing the descriptions. If pairs complete the activity, check student understanding by listening to the descriptions and looking at the drawings.

4. TPR Variation

Using Total Physical Response technique, introduce the imperatives listed below. Use motions and hand signals to show phrase meanings while students listen and watch. When you finish, have the students repeat the motions and the phrases.

Open your mouth.	Bend your ankle.
Say "ah."	Bend your elbow.
Make a fist.	Take a deep breath.
Lift your leg.	Swallow.
Bend your knee.	Bend your finger.
Lift your arm.	

You may have advanced students assume the role of doctor to give the instructions while other students show understanding by completing the actions.

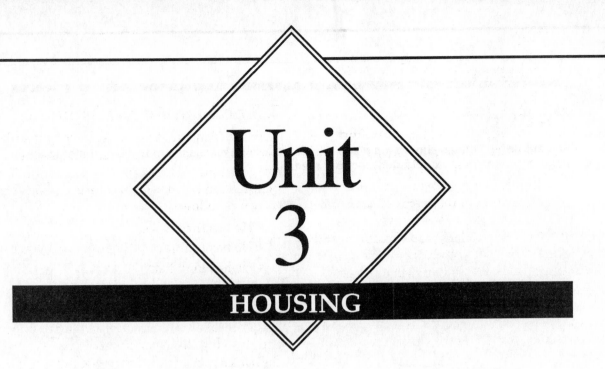

Picture It

The following pictures provide meaning for the life skills vocabulary used throughout the unit.

The illustrations in this unit show types of housing, rooms, furniture, and appliances. Housing management and repair personnel are also introduced. Familiarity with housing terms allows students to either secure housing or relocate successfully.

Rather than introducing all vocabulary items before beginning the exercises, refer to the pictures while students complete the unit. If all the vocabulary is introduced before beginning the unit, students will have difficulty remembering meaning, pronunciation, and usage. Introduce the words in the context of the unit activities. For example, before asking students to complete "Guess Who, Where, or What," use the pictures to show word meanings for the vocabulary in that exercise.

Pictures in the student's edition are not labeled. Learning meaning before seeing the written word facilitates comprehension and correct pronunciation. When introducing the vocabulary in the pictures, you may want to model each word and have the class repeat it after you. Give examples of the word in sentences. After meaning is clear and students can identify vocabulary items, they can label the pictures with your assistance. Once students have labeled the pictures, they can use this section to review word meaning and spelling.

Picture It

The following pictures show people and things that will be discussed in this unit. Refer to these pictures when doing exercises throughout the unit.

1. _floor lamp_   4. _arm chair_   7. _coffee table_
2. _window_   5. _television (T.V.)_
3. _end table_   6. _sofa_

1. _picture_   4. _dresser_   7. _crib_
2. _mirror_   5. _bed_
3. _closet_   6. _rug_

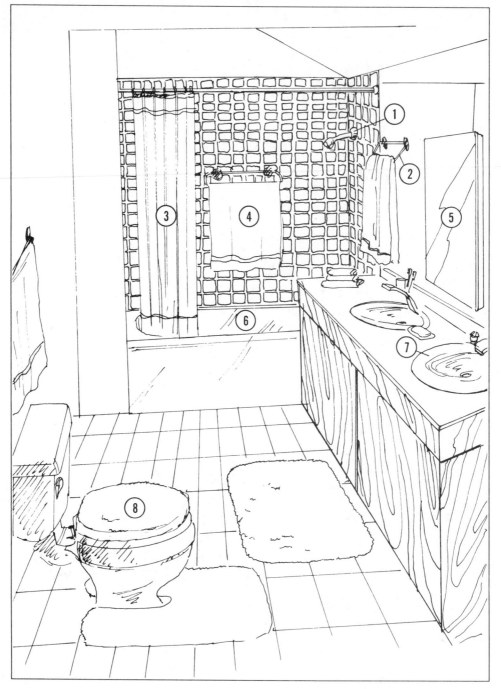

1. _shower_   4. _towel_   7. _sink_
2. _towel rack_   5. _medicine cabinet_ 8. _toilet_
3. _shower curtain_ 6. _bathtub_

1. _curtains_

2. _cabinets_

3. _sink_

4. _clock_

5. _refrigerator_

6. _stove_

7. _table_

1. _shelf_   3. _furnace_   5. _dryer_

2. _hot water heater_   4. _washer_   6. _stairs_

1. _light_   3. _place setting_   5. _chair_

2. _china cabinet_   4. _table_

1. *lawn furniture*

2. *attic*

3. *real estate agent*

4. *apartment*

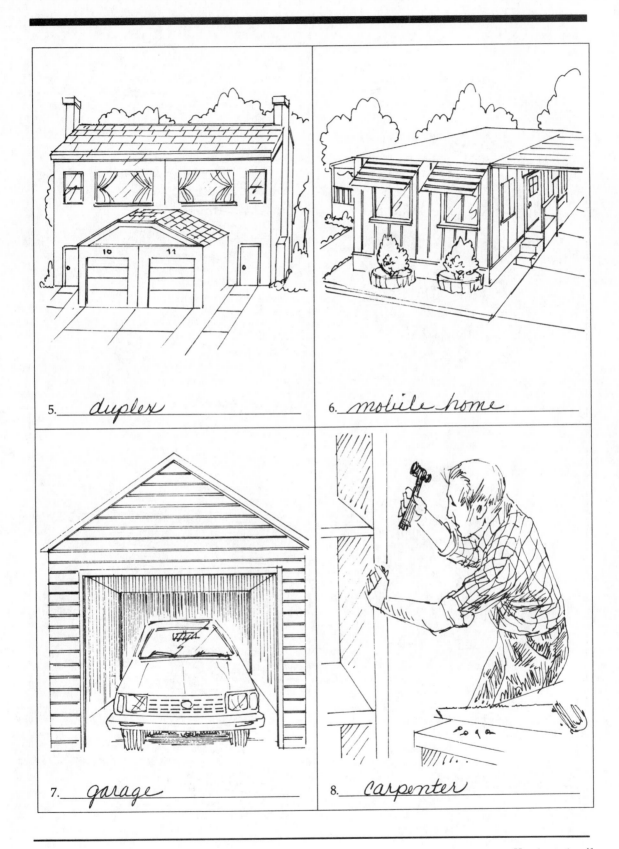

5. _duplex_

6. _mobile home_

7. _garage_

8. _carpenter_

9. *electrician*

10. *plumber*

11. *manager*

12. *ad*

Give It a Try

This exercise provides practice of words in context.

After word meaning is introduced through pictures, read each group of phrases orally with the students' books closed. After the students master the phrases, they can open their books and read the phrases together.

You may need to explain words unfamiliar to the students before beginning the exercise. Begin the oral presentation by modeling each phrase. Have the students repeat the phrase. Then give a cue word. The students repeat the sentence with the new cue word.

Give It a Try

Practice the phrases listed below.

1. _Oscar_ rents _an apartment_.
Carmen	a house
Susan	a mobile home
Ben	a townhouse
Anita	a duplex

2. The tenant called the _landlord_ for help. What did the _landlord_ say?
manager	manager
carpenter	carpenter
electrician	electrician
plumber	plumber

3. Please _paint_ the _bedroom_.
clean	bathroom
sweep	basement
vacuum	living room

4. We need _a rug_ for the _kitchen_.
a lamp	bedroom
towels	bathroom
chairs	living room

5. The _toilet_ is leaking.
   sink
   bathtub
   shower

6. Does your apartment have a _yard_? No, it doesn't.
   garage
   patio
   porch

7. The _door_ is broken.
   window
   hot water heater
   cabinet

Example:

Teacher: The toilet is leaking.

Students: The toilet is leaking.

Teacher: Sink.

Students: The sink is leaking.

Teacher: Bathtub.

Students: The bathtub is leaking.

Attention, Please!

This exercise provides practice in listening and reading.

Before asking students to complete this exercise, review prepositions of location (*on, in, around, over, under, beside, with, behind*).

Read each oral cue twice in normal speech. The cues are available only in the teacher's edition. Students listen to the cue, read the three choices in their books, and then circle the word or phrase identified by the cue. After the students complete the exercise, check their responses orally.

Attention, Please!

Listen to the teacher's cue. Then, circle the correct response.

1. blinds — (carpet) — ceiling
2. (refrigerator) — sofa — shower
3. picture — chair — (curtains)
4. (toilet) — crib — bed
5. dresser — sofa — (cabinets)
6. towel — (lamp) — ceiling
7. toilets — (chairs) — curtains
8. stoves — (shelves) — tables
9. (basement) — attic — garage
10. shower — (picture) — floor
11. (closet) — stove — sink
12. refrigerator — (end table) — sink

Teacher Cues

1. It's on the floor.
2. It's in the kitchen.
3. They're on the window.
4. It's in the bathroom.
5. They're over the sink.
6. It's beside the bed.
7. They're around the table.
8. They're in the cabinets.
9. It's under the house.
10. It's on the wall over the bed.
11. ~~It's behind the door.~~ where you hang your clothes
12. It's next to the sofa.

Tell Me About It

This is a pair activity. One student has information that another student needs, but doesn't have, in order to complete a task.

Before asking students to complete this exercise, you may want to review prepositions of location (*on, under, behind, next to, in, above,* etc.) and directional words (*left, right, straight, up,* and *down*).

Divide the class into pairs of students. One person in each pair uses Part A; the other uses Part B. Parts A and B are back-to-back pages in the student's edition. Partners should be seated so that they can't see each other's pages. Partners take turns asking questions about items in the pictures. Referring to the visual clues and using directional words, students answer each other's questions and write the new information in the correct places on the pictures.

Monitor the activity by listening to each pair of students. After students complete all the questions, ask them to check their communication by comparing Parts A and B.

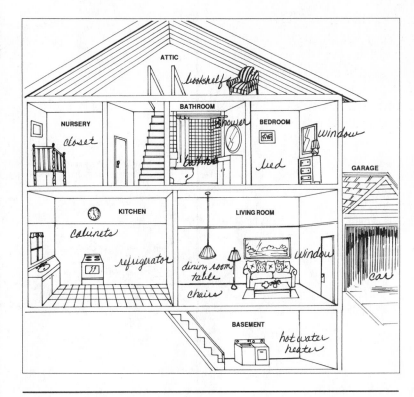

Tell Me About It (Part A)

Study the picture. Then, ask your partner the questions below. Using your partner's answers, write the name of each underlined item in the correct place on the picture.

Where's the closet?
Where's the refrigerator?
Where's the shower?
Where are the chairs?
Where's the hot water heater?
Where's the dining room table?
Where's the bookshelf?

Where's the window (upstairs)?
Where's the window (downstairs)?
Is there a car in the garage?
Is there a bed in the bedroom?
Is there a bathtub in the bathroom?
Are there cabinets in the kitchen?

Housing ◆ 45

Tell Me About It (Part B)

Study the picture. Then, ask your partner the questions below. Using your partner's answers, write the name of each underlined item in the correct place on the picture.

Where's the <u>dresser</u>?
Where's the <u>lamp</u>?
Where's the <u>dryer</u>?
Where's the <u>sink</u>?
Where's the <u>sofa</u>?
Where's the <u>floor lamp</u>?
Where's the <u>toilet</u>?

Where did they put the <u>crib</u>?
Where did they put the <u>clock</u>?
Where did they put the <u>picture</u>?
Where did they put the <u>stove</u>?
Where's the <u>old chair</u>?
Where's the <u>washer</u>?

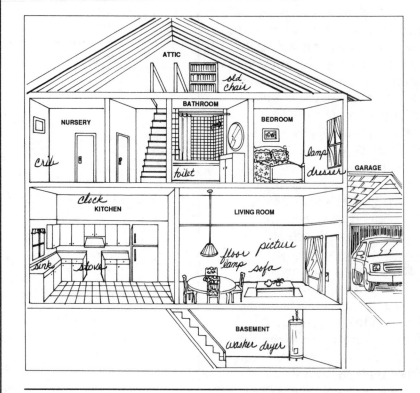

Guess Who, Where, or What

This is a category exercise that can be used with pairs of students in multilevel classes. It can also be completed by individual students. Having students list words under appropriate categories checks their understanding of word meanings.

Students read each word or phrase in the list and decide if it describes a person, place, or thing. Then each student writes the word or phrase in the correct category. You should categorize the first word to provide an example for the students.

Guess Who, Where, or What

Read each word or phrase in the list below. Ask a classmate if the word or phrase describes a person, place, or thing. Write the words in the correct category.

landlord
patio
super
window
real estate agent
manager
bedroom
garage
closet

kitchen
screen door
plumber
carpenter
electrician
bathroom
basement
ceiling
porch

walls
dining room
cabinets
floor
corner
living room
attic
hall

People Who Work in Housing	Places in a House	Parts of a Room
landlord	patio	window
super	bedroom	closet
real estate agent	garage	screen door
manager	kitchen	ceiling
plumber	bathroom	walls
carpenter	basement	cabinets
electrician	porch	corner
	dining room	floor
	living room	
	attic/hall	

Two Against One

This category exercise checks students' understanding of word meaning and usage.

Explain the concept of a set to the class before beginning the exercise.

Ask students to read the three words in each set and then circle the word that doesn't belong to the set. Check the exercise orally by asking students to explain their choices. More than one answer is acceptable in some exercise sets. The students' explanation of their choices determines acceptable answers.

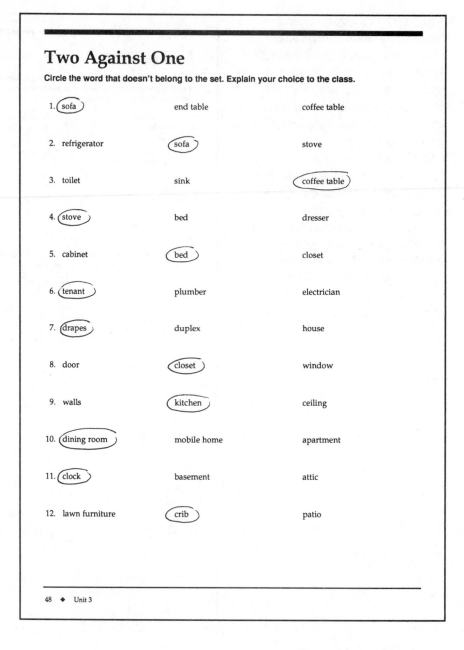

Two Against One

Circle the word that doesn't belong to the set. Explain your choice to the class.

1. (sofa)   end table   coffee table

2. refrigerator   (sofa)   stove

3. toilet   sink   (coffee table)

4. (stove)   bed   dresser

5. cabinet   (bed)   closet

6. (tenant)   plumber   electrician

7. (drapes)   duplex   house

8. door   (closet)   window

9. walls   (kitchen)   ceiling

10. (dining room)   mobile home   apartment

11. (clock)   basement   attic

12. lawn furniture   (crib)   patio

48   ◆   Unit 3

Inside Story

This activity facilitates students' use of contextual clues and provides practice in finding synonyms. Rather than just measuring basic comprehension of vocabulary, the exercise fosters the skill of analysis.

First ask the students to read the entire story. Then ask them to find words from the word list that have the same meanings as the words under the blank lines in the story. Instruct the students to write the matching words on the blanks. You may want to fill in the first blank to provide the students with an example. When all the matching words are found and all the blanks are filled in, students should read the story again using the new words.

Inside Story

Read the story below. Choose words or phrases from the list that have the same meanings as the words or phrases under the lines. Write the correct words on the blanks. Read the story again using the words written on the blanks.

deposit	Street	many	rent
walls	leaking	refrigerator	cabinets
excited	manager	an apartment	broken
kitchen	door	bedroom	carpet
ads	shower	very much	

Margaret's Decision

Margaret wanted to rent _an apartment_ . She looked at the
(small housing)

ads in the Sunday newspaper. There were
(advertisements)

many apartments!
(a lot of)

Margaret went to the apartment on 6th _Street_ . She asked the
(road)

manager to show her the apartment. She was _excited_
(supervisor)   (happy)

until the _door_ opened. The _kitchen_ was small. The
(entrance)   (cooking place)

cabinets were dirty and there was no _refrigerator_ . The
(cupboards)   (ice box)

bedroom window was _broken_ . The
(sleeping place)   (cracked)

shower was _leaking_ . The
(bathing place)   (dripping)

walls needed paint and the _carpet_ was dirty.
(room sides)   (rug)

The manager said the _rent_ was only $375.00 and the
(money paid each month)

deposit was only $200.00. Margaret said, "Thank you
(dollars paid before)

very much , but I need to look around."
(a lot)

Take Your Pick

This multiple choice exercise measures students' understanding of vocabulary meaning and usage in sentences.

Review the unit vocabulary using the pictures at the beginning of the unit. Explain any other new vocabulary in the exercise items before asking students to complete the exercise.

Tell the students to choose the word or phrase missing in each sentence from among the three choices listed under the sentence. Prefixes and suffixes that change word meaning appear in some of the answer choices. Have students write the missing word or phrase on the blank in each sentence.

Take Your Pick

There is a missing word or phrase in each sentence below. Read each sentence. Then, look at the three choices under the sentence. Choose the correct word or phrase and write it on the blank.

1. The _rent_ is too high.

   rental   renting   rent

2. The _plumber_ came to fix the bathroom sink.

   electrician   plumber   carpenter

3. Juana needs a(n) _carpenter_ to put new cabinets in the kitchen.

   electrician   plumber   carpenter

4. Why don't you ask the _electrician_ ?

   electric   electrician   electricity

5. The _wall_ is cracked.

   wall   carpet   curtains

6. Sarah needs help. The toilet is _leaking_ .

   leaking   leak   leaked

7. The closet _door_ is broken.

   drawer   table   door

8. Juan looked up and saw that the _ceiling_ was cracked.

   floor   ceiling   rug

9. She had to pay rent and a _damage deposit_ on the first of the month.

   apartment   damage deposit   lease

10. It was a beautiful summer day, so they decided to eat on the _patio_ .

    kitchen   patio   basement

Bingo

1. Make the bingo cards.

Students create bingo cards through teacher dictation of vocabulary. The dictation provides a spelling assessment as well as a listening activity.

Instruct the students to look at the empty bingo grid in their book. The grid has nine squares for nine vocabulary items. Read the vocabulary to the class. Ask students to write the words in the boxes at random, not in rows. Each student should have a different bingo card after nine items are dictated.

2. Check students' spelling.

When the bingo cards are completed, write the vocabulary words on the board and ask students to check their spelling and make corrections.

3. Play bingo.

Distribute eight markers — such as paper clips, buttons, chips, or pennies — to each student. Read each oral cue twice in normal speech. Students find the corresponding vocabulary item on their cards and cover it with a marker. When one student has three in a row, he or she calls "bingo" and then reads off the words in the marked squares for checking. You may need to demonstrate how bingo is played for those students who have never played before.

There are two game options. Choose the one that best fits the students' level of proficiency, or use them both at different times of instruction.

Game 1

Vocabulary for Dictation	Teacher Cues
tenant	She pays the rent.
carpenter	He fixes cabinets.
plumber	She fixes leaky pipes.
door	It opens and closes.
landlord	She collects the rent.
bedroom	For sleeping.
ad	Something you read to find an apartment.
duplex	Two houses together.
kitchen	A place for cooking.

Game 2

Vocabulary for Dictation	Teacher Cues
manager	I need a damage deposit.
rent	Three hundred and fifty dollars.
leaky faucet	It drips.
washer and dryer	In the laundry room.
attic	Upstairs.
basement	Downstairs.
broken window	It's cracked.
drapes	Something you put on a window.
rug	Something you put on a floor.

Get It Together

The crossword puzzle provides practice in recognizing word meaning and usage.

Have students read each numbered clue and write the answer in the puzzle spaces with the same number. A word list of answers is given so that spelling will not hinder students' ability to complete the puzzle.

To quiz the spelling skills of more advanced students, ask the students to cover the word list while filling in the puzzle squares.

Get It Together

There is a word missing in each sentence below. Choose the correct word from the word list. Print that word in the boxes of the puzzle.

attic	living room	bathroom
manager	corner	tenant
door	yard	garage
rug	rent	kitchen

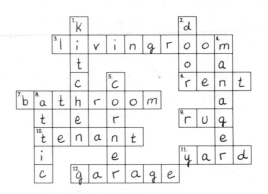

Across

3. He's in the _____ resting on the sofa.

6. Pay the _____ on the first of the month.

7. The toilet in the _____ upstairs is broken.

9. The new _____ is on the floor in the bedroom.

10. The _____ pays the rent.

11. She plants flowers in the _____ .

12. The car is in the _____ .

Down

1. He's in the _____ making lunch.

2. The _____ is locked.

4. The _____ collects the rent.

5. Put the table in the _____ of the room.

8. The _____ is the top floor of a house.

And There's More

1. Concentration

Copy and cut out individual pictures from the beginning of the unit. Mount the pictures on 3" x 5" cards. Label the back of the pictures with consecutive numbers. On an equal number of cards, write the names of the pictures. Then label the back of the cards with consecutive letters.

Lay all the cards on a large table, pictures and words facing down. Ask students to take turns choosing two cards, trying to match a picture with its word. Ask each student to read the word and identify the picture on the card he or she chooses. Then the student decides if the cards are a match. Check to be sure the student's decision is correct.

If there is no match, the cards are turned back over. If there is a match, the student keeps the pair of cards. The winner is the person who has the most matched cards.

Concentration helps exercise memory, gives review of letter and number names, and reinforces vocabulary.

2. Memory Circle

Have students sit in a circle and ask each to name a household item that needs to be fixed. You should start the dialogue by naming an item. The first student repeats the item you have named and adds another item. As the game continues, each student repeats what has been said, then adds a piece of furniture or room of the house of his or her choice. Items may or may not be given in alphabetical order. Here's an example of how the activity should progress:

Teacher:	I need to fix the armchair.
First student:	I need to fix the armchair and the bathtub.
Second student:	I need to fix the armchair, the bathtub, and the closet.

In multilevel classes beginners should start the process and more advanced students should follow, so that the advanced students have to remember more items.

3. Write an Ad

Ask students to imagine that they own a house or an apartment building. Ask them to write newspaper ads to sell their property. Before giving this assignment introduce abbreviations used in ads. Here are some examples of common abbreviations:

furn.(furnished)	AC(air conditioning)
dep.(deposit)	apt.(apartment)
mo.(month)	gar.(garage)
bdrm.(bedroom)	unfurn.(unfurnished)

4. Pick a Problem

On small cards write problems that need to be reported to a landlord or supervisor. Here are some examples of problems:

a leaking toilet	a dripping pipe
a leaking faucet	a torn carpet
a cracked ceiling	a broken cabinet
a broken window	

Divide the class into pairs of students. Ask each pair to choose a card. Then ask each pair to role play a situation between a tenant and a landlord or supervisor. Tell the students that one person in each pair should play a tenant reporting the problem written on their card to the landlord or supervisor. The other should play the landlord or supervisor.

Ask for volunteers to present their role play to the class.

Unit 4

AMERICAN GOVERNMENT

Picture It

The following pictures provide meaning for the life skills vocabulary used throughout the unit.

Concepts of citizenship and government as practiced in the United States are illustrated in this unit. Concepts include voting, the American flag and other patriotic symbols that students need to recognize, the three branches of American government, and government officials. A map of the world and a map of the fifty states put the nation's capital in geographical perspective for students.

Explain to students that Supreme Court judges are usually called justices. You may also want to identify the fifty states.

Rather than introducing all vocabulary items before beginning the exercises, refer to the pictures while students complete the unit. If all the vocabulary is introduced before beginning the unit, students will have difficulty

remembering meaning, pronunciation, and usage. Introduce the words in the context of the unit activities. For example, before asking students to complete "Guess Who, Where, or What," use the pictures to show word meanings for the vocabulary in that exercise.

Pictures in the student's edition are not labeled. Learning meaning before seeing the written word facilitates comprehension and correct pronunciation. When introducing the vocabulary in the pictures, you may want to model each word and have the class repeat it after you. Give examples of the word in sentences. After meaning is clear and students can identify vocabulary items, they can label the pictures with your assistance. Once students have labeled the pictures, they can use this section to review word meaning and spelling.

Picture It

The following pictures show people and things that will be discussed in this unit. Refer to these pictures when doing exercises throughout the unit.

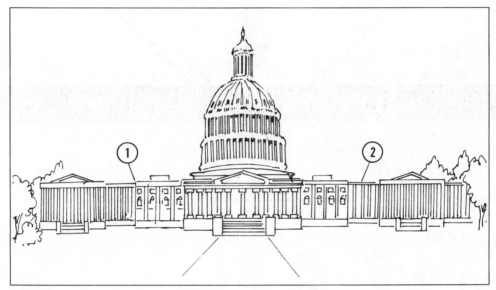

1. _Senate_   2. _House of Representatives_

1. _president_   2. _White House_

1. _Supreme Court_

2. _judge_

3. _voter_

4. bald eagle

5. George Washington

6. president

7. vice-president

8. senator

9. representative

10. American flag

11. Star Spangled Banner

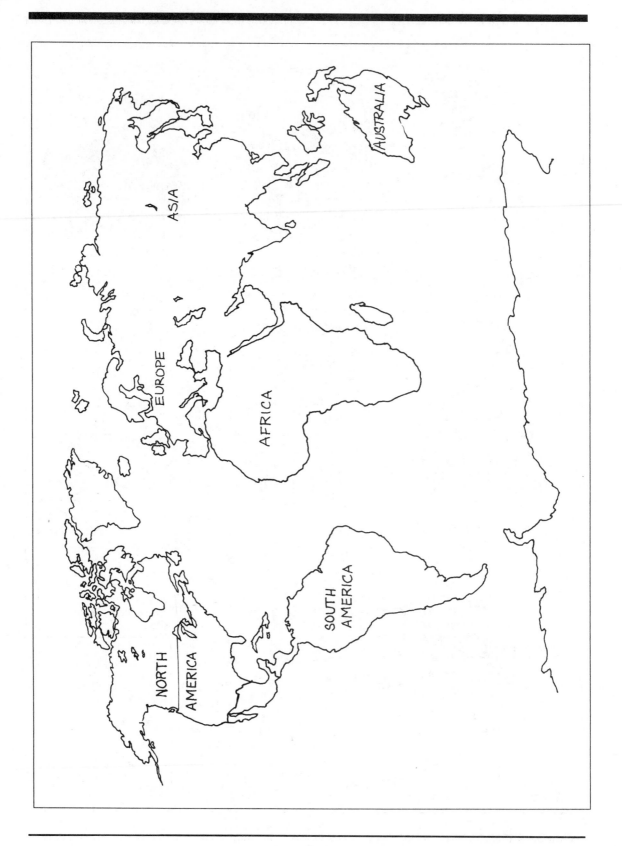

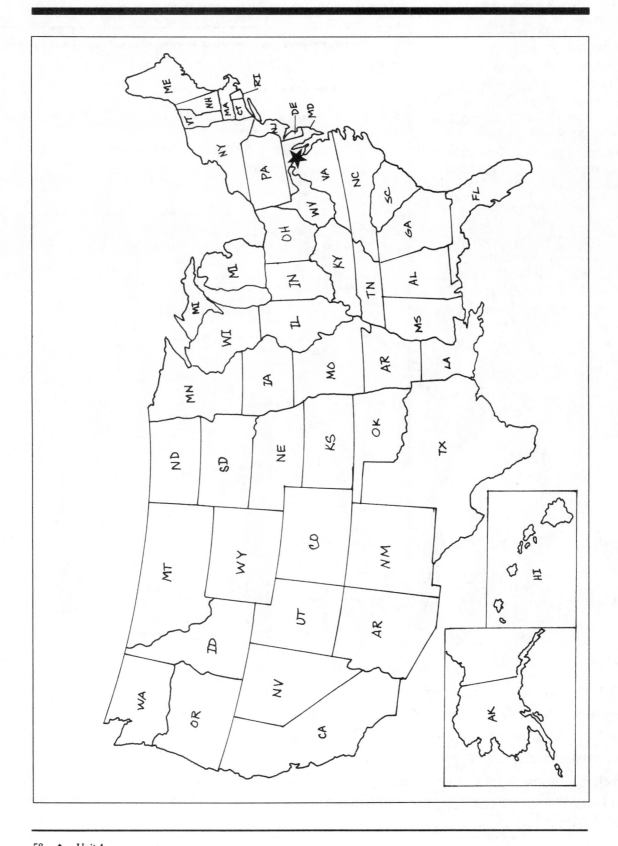

Give It a Try

This exercise provides practice of words in context.

After word meaning is introduced through pictures, read each group of phrases orally with the students' books closed. After the students master the phrases, they can open their books and read the phrases together.

You may need to explain words unfamiliar to the students before beginning the exercise. Begin the oral presentation by modeling each phrase. Have the students repeat the phrase. Then give a cue word. The students repeat the sentence with the new cue word.

Give It a Try

Practice the phrases listed below.

1. The _eagle_ is a symbol of __the country__ .
   flag   the nation
   anthem   the United States

2. The people of the _nation_ are the voters.
           state
           city
           U.S.

3. How many _stars_ does the flag have? It has _50_ .
       stripes   13
       colors   3

4. The flag is sometimes called _____Old Glory_____ .
           the Stars and Stripes
           the Star Spangled Banner

5. Who _is_ the __vice-president__ of the United States?
           president
   are   Supreme Court judges
           senators

6. We heard the __president's speech__ on the radio. _Who_ is the _____president_____ ?
       national anthem   What   national anthem
       Star Spangled Banner   What   Star Spangled Banner
       senator's speech   Who   senator

7. The __senator__ works in the _legislative_ branch.
   representative   legislative
   president   executive
   judge   judicial

8. Where is the _____White House_____ ? It's in Washington, D.C.
       Congress
       Supreme Court building
       Capitol building

Example:

Teacher: The eagle is a symbol of the country.

Students: The eagle is a symbol of the country.

Teacher: Flag, the nation.

Students: The flag is a symbol of the nation.

Teacher: Anthem, the United States.

Students: The anthem is a symbol of the United States.

Attention, Please!

This exercise provides practice in listening and reading.

Read each oral cue twice in normal speech. The cues are available only in the teacher's edition. Students listen to the cue, read the three choices in their books, and then circle the word or phrase identified by the cue. After the students complete the exercise, check their responses orally.

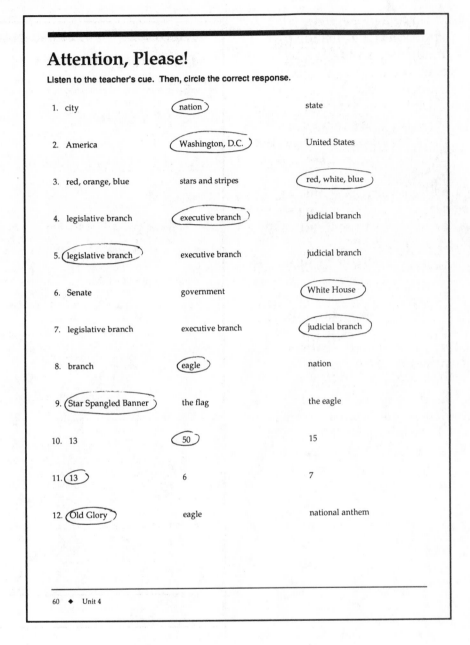

Attention, Please!

Listen to the teacher's cue. Then, circle the correct response.

1. city   (nation)   state

2. America   (Washington, D.C.)   United States

3. red, orange, blue   stars and stripes   (red, white, blue)

4. legislative branch   (executive branch)   judicial branch

5. (legislative branch)   executive branch   judicial branch

6. Senate   government   (White House)

7. legislative branch   executive branch   (judicial branch)

8. branch   (eagle)   nation

9. (Star Spangled Banner)   the flag   the eagle

10. 13   (50)   15

11. (13)   6   7

12. (Old Glory)   eagle   national anthem

60 ◆ Unit 4

Teacher Cues

1. The United States.
2. The national capital.
3. The colors of the flag.
4. The president and the vice-president.
5. Congress.
6. The president's home.
7. The Supreme Court.
8. A symbol of the United States.
9. The national anthem.
10. The number of stars on the American flag.
11. The number of stripes on the American flag.
12. Another name for the American flag.

Tell Me About It

This is a pair activity. One student has information that another student needs, but doesn't have, in order to complete a task.

Divide the class into pairs of students. One person in each pair uses Part A; the other uses Part B. Parts A and B are back-to-back pages in the student's edition. Partners should be seated so that they can't see each other's pages. Partners take turns asking questions about items in the pictures. Referring to the visual clues and using directional words, students answer each other's questions and write the new information in the correct places on the pictures.

Monitor the activity by listening to each pair of students. After students complete all the questions, ask them to check their communication by comparing Parts A and B.

Tell Me About It (Part A)

Study the picture. Then, ask your partner the questions below. Using your partner's answers, write the name of each underlined item in the correct place on the picture.

Where is the senator?
Where is the vice-president?
Where is the White House?

Where is the president?
Where is the House of Representatives?

NORTH

senator

REPRESENTATIVE

House of Representatives

WEST

EAST

president
White House

PENNSYLVANIA AVE.

vice-president

INDEPENDENCE AVE.

SOUTH

American Government ◆ 61

Tell Me About It (Part B)

Study the picture. Then, ask your partner the questions below. Using your partner's answers, write the name of each underlined item in the correct place on the picture.

Where is the <u>American flag</u>?   Where is the <u>representative</u>?
Where is the <u>Supreme Court</u>?   Where is the <u>Senate</u>?
Where is the <u>judge</u>?

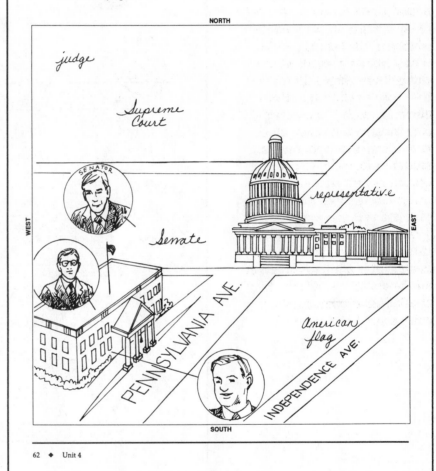

Guess Who, Where, or What

This is a category exercise that can be used with pairs of students in multilevel classes. It can also be completed by individual students. Having students list words under appropriate categories checks their understanding of word meanings.

Students read each word or phrase in the list and decide if it describes a person, place, or thing. Then each student writes the word or phrase in the correct category. You should categorize the first word to provide an example for the students.

Guess Who, Where, or What

Read each word or phrase in the list below. Ask a classmate if the word or phrase describes a person, place, or thing. Write the words in the correct category.

senator
Washington, D.C.
flag
Star Spangled Banner
state capital
voter
banner
vice-president

White House
president
House of Representatives
Senate
representative
national anthem
stripes

Congress
judge
stars
Supreme Court
eagle
national capital
colors

People in Government	Places in Government	Symbols of the Country
senator	Washington, D.C.	flag
voter	state capital	Star Spangled Banner
vice-president	White House	banner
president	House of Representatives	national anthem
representative	Senate	stripes
judge	Congress	stars
	Supreme Court	eagle
	national capital	colors

Two Against One

This category exercise checks students' understanding of word meaning and usage.

Explain the concept of a set to the class before beginning the exercise.

Ask students to read the three words in each set and then circle the word that doesn't belong to the set. Check the exercise orally by asking students to explain their choices. More than one answer is acceptable in some exercise sets. The students' explanation of their choices determines acceptable answers.

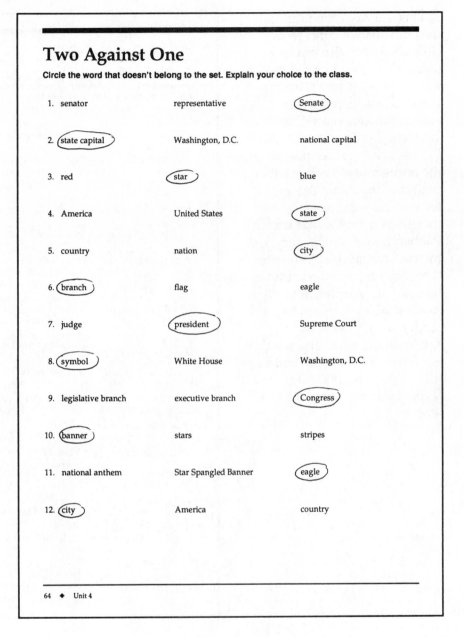

Two Against One

Circle the word that doesn't belong to the set. Explain your choice to the class.

1. senator   representative   (Senate)

2. (state capital)   Washington, D.C.   national capital

3. red   (star)   blue

4. America   United States   (state)

5. country   nation   (city)

6. (branch)   flag   eagle

7. judge   (president)   Supreme Court

8. (symbol)   White House   Washington, D.C.

9. legislative branch   executive branch   (Congress)

10. (banner)   stars   stripes

11. national anthem   Star Spangled Banner   (eagle)

12. (city)   America   country

Inside Story

This activity facilitates students' use of contextual clues and provides practice in finding synonyms. Rather than just measuring basic comprehension of vocabulary, the exercise fosters the skill of analysis.

First ask the students to read the entire story. Then ask them to find words from the word list that have the same meanings as the words under the blank lines in the story. Instruct the students to write the matching words on the blanks. You may want to fill in the first blank to provide the students with an example. When all the matching words are found and all the blanks are filled in, students should read the story again using the new words.

Inside Story

Read the story below. Choose words or phrases from the list that have the same meanings as the words or phrases under the lines. Write the correct words on the blanks. Read the story again using the words written on the blanks.

original	country	number
sometimes	anthem	3
the U.S.	national	flag
represent	coins	stripes
6	50	Spangled
symbol		

Symbols of America

The American ___*flag*___ is a symbol of our
(banner)

___*country*___. The flag has ___*3*___ colors. The colors
(nation)   (three)

are red, white, and blue. There are ___*50*___ stars on the flag. The stars
(fifty)

___*represent*___ the ___*number*___ of states in
(stand for)   (no.)

___*the U.S.*___. There are 7 red ___*stripes*___ and
(America)   (lines)

___*6*___ white stripes. The stripes represent the thirteen
(six)

___*original*___ states. The flag is ___*sometimes*___ called Old
(first)   (often)

Glory or the Stars and Stripes.

The national ___*anthem*___ was written by Francis Scott Key in 1814. The
(song)

national anthem is called the "Star ___*Spangled*___ Banner." People sing this song at
(spotted)

___*national*___ celebrations and at the beginning of sports events.
(country-wide)

The bald eagle is another ___*symbol*___ of America. The eagle is printed on
(sign)

___*coins*___ and bills.
(change)

Take Your Pick

This multiple choice exercise measures students' understanding of vocabulary meaning and usage in sentences.

Review the unit vocabulary using the pictures at the beginning of the unit. Explain any other new vocabulary in the exercise items before asking students to complete the exercise.

Tell the students to choose the word or phrase missing in each sentence from among the three choices listed under the sentence. Prefixes and suffixes that change word meaning appear in some of the answer choices. Have students write the missing word or phrase on the blank in each sentence.

Take Your Pick

There is a missing word or phrase in each sentence below. Read each sentence. Then, look at the three choices under the sentence. Choose the correct word or phrase and write it on the blank.

1. There are three branches of _American_ government.

   Americans   American   America

2. The _national_ anthem is the "Star Spangled Banner."

   national   nation   country

3. What are the three branches of _government_ ?

   governor   govern   government

4. _Senators_ make laws in congress.

   Senate   Senators   Senator

5. Congress has two houses, the Senate and the House of _Representatives_ .

   representative   represent   Representatives

6. The _legislative_ branch makes the laws.

   legislative   legislature   legislate

7. The _executive_ branch enforces the law.

   executives   judicial   executive

8. The Supreme Court is in the _judicial_ branch.

   judge   judicial   judging

9. There are _fifty_ stars on the flag.

   fifteen   thirteen   fifty

10. The president lives in the _White House_ in Washington, D.C.

    White House   White Home   Congress

Bingo

1. Make the bingo cards.

Students create bingo cards through teacher dictation of vocabulary. The dictation provides a spelling assessment as well as a listening activity.

Instruct the students to look at the empty bingo grid in their book. The grid has nine squares for nine vocabulary items. Read the vocabulary to the class. Ask students to write the words in the boxes at random, not in rows. Each student should have a different bingo card after nine items are dictated.

2. Check students' spelling.

When the bingo cards are completed, write the vocabulary words on the board and ask students to check their spelling and make corrections.

3. Play bingo.

Distribute eight markers — such as paper clips, buttons, chips, or pennies — to each student. Read each oral cue twice in normal speech. Students find the corresponding vocabulary item on their cards and cover it with a marker. When one student has three in a row, he or she calls "bingo" and then reads off the words in the marked squares for checking. You may need to demonstrate how bingo is played for those students who have never played before.

There are two game options. Choose the one that best fits the students' level of proficiency, or use them both at different times of instruction.

Game 1

Vocabulary for Dictation	Teacher Cues
stars	There are fifty on the flag.
stripes	There are thirteen on the flag.
colors	Red, white, and blue.
Old Glory	Another name for the American flag.
senator	He helps make the laws.
White House	The president lives here.
Washington D.C.	The nation's capital.
eagle	The national bird.
flag	A banner.

Game 2

Vocabulary for Dictation	Teacher Cues
legislative branch	Makes the laws.
executive branch	Enforces the laws.
judicial branch	Interprets the laws.
flag	Stars and stripes.
Supreme Court	The highest court.
Star Spangled Banner	The national anthem.
George Washington	The first president.
country	Nation.
states	Colorado, California, and New York.

Get It Together

The crossword puzzle provides practice in recognizing word meaning and usage.

Have students read each numbered clue and write the answer in the puzzle spaces with the same number. A word list of answers is given so that spelling will not hinder students' ability to complete the puzzle.

To quiz the spelling skills of more advanced students, ask the students to cover the word list while filling in the puzzle squares.

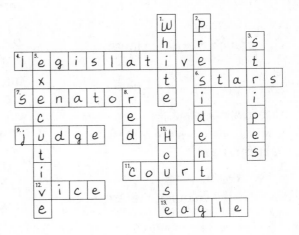

Get It Together

There is a word missing in each sentence below. Choose the correct word from the word list. Print that word in the boxes of the puzzle.

legislative
eagle
White
president
judge

Court
stars
House
red

vice
stripes
senator
executive

Across

4. The _____ branch makes the laws.

6. There are 50 _____ on the flag.

7. A _____ works in the Senate.

9. A _____ works in the Supreme Court.

11. The Supreme _____ is the judicial branch.

12. The _____ -president helps the president.

13. The _____ is a national emblem.

Down

1. The president lives in the _____ House.

2. The first _____ was George Washington.

3. There are 13 _____ on the flag.

5. The president is in the _____ branch.

8. The flag colors are _____ , white, and blue.

10. The president lives in the White _____ .

68 ◆ Unit 4

And There's More

1. Some Answers, Some Questions

In this activity you present the answers to some questions and the students must provide the questions that match the answers. Call on individual students to respond. Here are some examples:

Teacher: George Washington
Student: Who was the first president?

Teacher: legislative branch
Student: What branch makes the laws?

Teacher: eagle
Student: What is the national bird?

Teacher: thirteen stripes
Student: How many stripes are on the American flag?

Teacher: red, white, and blue
Student: What are the colors of the American flag?

Teacher: executive branch
Student: What branch enforces the law?

Teacher: Star Spangled Banner
Student: What is the national anthem?

There are many possibilities for teacher answers and student questions. Use questions from the United States citizenship examination.

2. Home Country Flags

Divide the class into pairs of students. If possible, pairs should be made up of students from different countries.

Each person in the pair describes his or her national flag to his or her partner. The partner's task is to draw the flag described. Students may use bilingual dictionaries if needed. Flag descriptions should include colors, numbers, and shapes.

3. The Perfect Government

This activity is appropriate for high intermediate or advanced students. Ask them to create the perfect government for an unknown country. Using labeled diagrams or written and oral descriptions, students describe the make-believe government.

The description should include some of the following topics:

- leadership
- how leadership is chosen
- how many leaders are necessary
- how laws are made
- who makes the laws
- the role of the people in the country
- division of power

After students complete the assignment, they can share their descriptions with the class. The activity also can be completed in small groups of three or four students.

4. Tic-Tac-Toe

Prepare a grid as shown below on the board. The same grid can be produced on an overhead transparency using pictures from the beginning of the unit. Copy the pictures, cut them out, and glue each picture onto a grid square.

1. Star Spangled Banner	2. Congress	3. vice-president of the United States
4. judical branch	5. executive branch	6. George Washington
7. president of the United States	8. eagle	9. legislative branch

Divide the class into two teams, Team *X* and Team *O*. Each person on a team has a chance to choose a square and tell the meaning of the word or phrase inside the square. If the person answers correctly, his or her team gets an *X* or *O* in that square. A team wins when there are three *X*'s or *O*'s in a row. Here's an example of how you might proceed:

Teacher: Choose a square.

Student: I choose number two. Congress is the Senate and the House of Representatives.

Teacher: Correct. You get an *X*.

Some students may not be familiar with the game of tic-tac-toe. Play the game on the board using only *X* and *O* before trying the game described here.

Do 1st

Picture It

The following pictures provide meaning for the life skills vocabulary used throughout the unit.

In this unit, students become familiar with food items commonly seen in American supermarkets. The presentation of food items, supermarket sections, and market personnel are depicted. Knowledge of food names and shopping terms, such as *aisle* and *sale*, enables students to ask where items are located and to shop efficiently.

Rather than introducing all vocabulary items before beginning the exercises, refer to the pictures while students complete the unit. If all the vocabulary is introduced before beginning the unit, students will have difficulty remembering meaning, pronunciation, and usage. Introduce the words in the context of the unit activities. For example, before asking students to complete "Guess Who, Where, or What," use the pictures to show word meanings for the vocabulary in that exercise.

Pictures in the student's edition are not labeled. Learning meaning before seeing the written word facilitates comprehension and correct pronunciation. When introducing the vocabulary in the pictures, you may want to model each word and have the class repeat it after you. Give examples of the word in sentences. After meaning is clear and students can identify vocabulary items, they can label the pictures with your assistance. Once students have labeled the pictures, they can use this section to review word meaning and spelling.

Picture It

The following pictures show people and things that will be discussed in this unit. Refer to these pictures when doing exercises throughout the unit.

1. *sale sign*   2. *shopping cart*   3. *aisle*

1. *store manager*   3. *check-out stand*   5. *sacker*
2. *fast lane*   4. *cashier*

1. *produce section*

2. *dairy section*

3. *bakery*

4. _deli_

5. _meat and poultry section_

6. _frozen foods_

7. *canned foods*

8. *paper products*

9. *beverage section*

10. *jar*

11. *sack*

12. *bottle*

13. *dozen*

14. *bag*

15. *box*

16. *can*

17. *package*

18. *carton*

19. *receipt*

20. *ad*

74 ◆ Unit 5

Give It a Try

This exercise provides practice of words in context.

After word meaning is introduced through pictures, read each group of phrases orally with the students' books closed. After the students master the phrases, they can open their books and read the phrases together.

You may need to explain words unfamiliar to the students before beginning the exercise. Begin the oral presentation by modeling each phrase. Have the students repeat the phrase. Then give a cue word. The students repeat the sentence with the new cue word.

Give It a Try

Practice the phrases listed below.

1. Is <u>cereal</u> on sale today? Yes, it's 10% off.
   rice
   flour

2. Where is the <u>canned fruit</u>? It's on aisle 3.
   spaghetti
   soup
   hot sauce

3. I have to return this <u>milk</u>. It's spoiled.
   cheese
   butter
   fish

4. The <u>cashier</u> works until <u>7:00</u> tonight. How late <u>do you</u> work?
   manager   7:30   does Rosa
   clerk   10:00   does Patrick

5. The <u>tomatoes</u> are in the <u>produce section</u>.
   napkins   paper products section
   chicken   meat section
   donuts   bakery

6. Where is the <u>produce section</u>?
   paper products section
   meat section
   bakery

7. I'm going to the <u>beverage</u> section. I need <u>a soda</u>.
   dairy   milk
   frozen food   ice cream
   meat   hamburger

8. I bought a <u>box</u> of <u>peas</u>.
   can   corn
   bottle ketchup
   jar   jelly

Example:

Teacher: I bought a box of peas.

Students: I bought a box of peas.

Teacher: Can, corn.

Students: I bought a can of corn.

Teacher: Bottle, ketchup.

Students: I bought a bottle of ketchup.

Attention, Please!

This exercise provides practice in listening and reading.

Before asking students to complete the exercise, review packages and weights using the pictures at the beginning of the unit.

Read each oral cue twice in normal speech. The cues are available only in the teacher's edition. Students listen to the cue, read the three choices in their books, and then circle the word or phrase identified by the cue. After the students complete the exercise, check their responses orally.

Attention, Please!

Listen to the teacher's cue. Then, circle the correct response.

1.	eggs	(flour)	soup
2.	bread	coffee	(cereal)
3.	eggs	crackers	(milk)
4.	(spaghetti)	oranges	apples
5.	potato chips	(soup)	bread
6.	apples	orange juice	(jelly)
7.	milk	orange juice	(hamburger)
8.	orange juice	coffee	(bread)
9.	cottage cheese	(eggs)	butter
10.	(carrots)	milk	cereal
11.	napkins	(oil)	bread
12.	(butter)	ketchup	flour

76 ◆ Unit 5

Teacher Cues

1. I need five pounds.
2. I need two boxes.
3. I need one quart.
4. I need one package.
5. I need three cans.
6. I need one jar.
7. I need one pound.
8. I need one loaf.
9. I need one dozen.
10. I need two pounds.
11. I need a sixteen ounce bottle.
12. I need a stick.

Tell Me About It

This is a pair activity. One student has information that another student needs, but doesn't have, in order to complete a task.

Divide the class into pairs of students. One person in each pair uses Part A; the other uses Part B. Parts A and B are back-to-back pages in the student's edition. Partners should be seated so that they can't see each other's pages. Partners take turns asking questions about items in the pictures. Referring to the visual clues and using directional words, students answer each other's questions and write the new information in the correct places on the pictures.

Monitor the activity by listening to each pair of students. After students complete all the questions, ask them to check their communication by comparing Parts A and B.

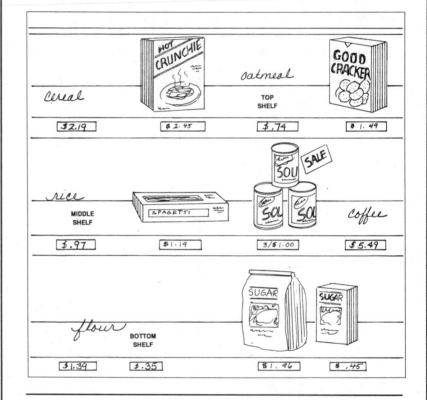

Tell Me About It (Part A)

Study the picture. Then, ask your partner the questions below. Using your partner's answers, write the name and price of each underlined item in the correct place on the picture.

Where's the <u>flour</u>?
Where's the <u>oatmeal</u>?
Where's the <u>rice</u>?
Where's the <u>coffee</u>?
Where's the <u>cereal</u>?
What's on sale today?

How much is the <u>flour</u>?
How much is the <u>oatmeal</u>?
How much is the <u>rice</u>?
How much is the <u>coffee</u>?
How much is the <u>cereal</u>?

Tell Me About It (Part B)

Study the picture. Then, ask your partner the questions below. Using your partner's answers, write the name and price of each underlined item in the correct place on the picture.

Where's the soup?	How much is the soup?
Where's the spaghetti?	How much is the spaghetti?
Where's the sugar?	How much is the sugar?
Where's the hot cereal?	How much is the hot cereal?
Where are the crackers?	How much are the crackers?
What's on sale today?	

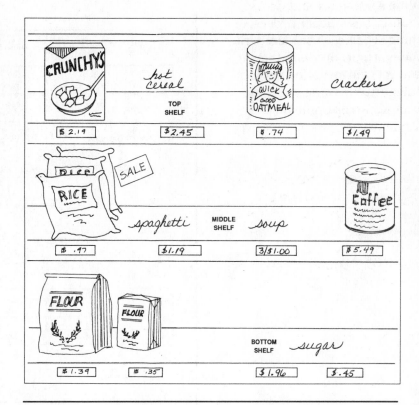

Guess Who, Where, or What

This is a category exercise that can be used with pairs of students in multilevel classes. It can also be completed by individual students. Having students list words under appropriate categories checks their understanding of word meanings.

Students read each word or phrase in the list and decide if it describes a person, place, or thing. Then each student writes the word or phrase in the correct category. You should categorize the first word to provide an example for the students.

Guess Who, Where, or What

Read each word or phrase in the list below. Ask a classmate if the word or phrase describes a person, place, or thing. Write the words in the correct category.

cashier	manager	produce
milk	deli	bakery
eggs	flour	rice
meats	frozen foods	sugar
canned foods	paper products	napkins
sacker	butcher	dairy
oranges	butter	

People Who Work in the Supermarket	Sections of the Supermarket	Things to Buy at the Supermarket
cashier	canned foods	milk
sacker	deli	eggs
manager	frozen foods	meats
butcher	paper products	oranges
	produce	flour
	bakery	butter
	dairy	rice
		sugar
		napkins

Two Against One

This category exercise checks students' understanding of word meaning and usage.

Explain the concept of a set to the class before beginning the exercise.

Ask students to read the three words in each set and then circle the word that doesn't belong to the set. Check the exercise orally by asking students to explain their choices. More than one answer is acceptable in some exercise sets. The students' explanation of their choices determines acceptable answers.

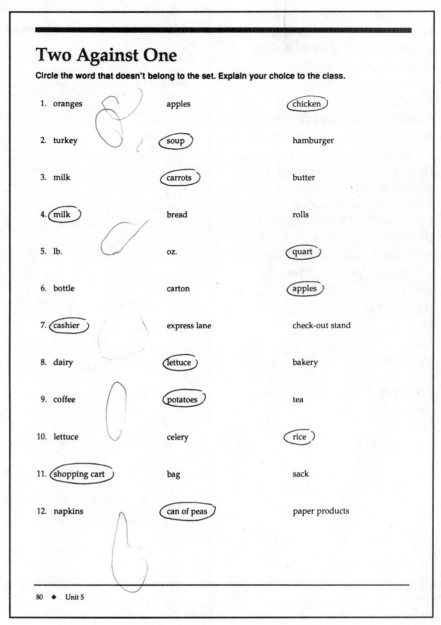

Two Against One

Circle the word that doesn't belong to the set. Explain your choice to the class.

1. oranges   apples   (chicken)

2. turkey   (soup)   hamburger

3. milk   (carrots)   butter

4. (milk)   bread   rolls

5. lb.   oz.   (quart)

6. bottle   carton   (apples)

7. (cashier)   express lane   check-out stand

8. dairy   (lettuce)   bakery

9. coffee   (potatoes)   tea

10. lettuce   celery   (rice)

11. (shopping cart)   bag   sack

12. napkins   (can of peas)   paper products

80   ◆   Unit 5

Inside Story

This activity facilitates students' use of contextual clues and provides practice in finding synonyms. Rather than just measuring basic comprehension of vocabulary, the exercise fosters the skill of analysis.

First ask the students to read the entire story. Then ask them to find words from the word list that have the same meanings as the words under the blank lines in the story. Instruct the students to write the matching words on the blanks. You may want to fill in the first blank to provide the students with an example. When all the matching words are found and all the blanks are filled in, students should read the story again using the new words.

Inside Story

Read the story below. Choose words or phrases from the list that have the same meanings as the words or phrases under the lines. Write the correct words on the blanks. Read the story again using the words written on the blanks.

cashier	sacks	sale
dairy	shopping	hungry
pounds	bakery	supermarket
40	produce	check-out lane
groceries	list	shopping cart

Shopping with Kien

Kien needed ___*groceries*___ , so he went ___*shopping*___
          (food)   (to buy food)

after work. When Kien went inside the ___*supermarket*___ he noticed that he forgot his
                        (food store)

___*list*___ . He thought he could remember what he needed.
    (notes)

Kien walked to the ___*produce*___ section and put apples, oranges, and carrots
                (fruit and vegetable)

in his ___*shopping cart*___ . Then he went to the ___*bakery*___ for
     (basket)   (bread section)

bread, the ___*dairy*___ section for cheese and to the meat section for two
       (milk products)

___*pounds*___ of hamburger.
    (lbs.)

There was a ___*sale*___ on ice cream and on pizza. Kien didn't need ice
     (bargain)

cream or pizza, but he was ___*hungry*___ . After ___*40*___
                (starving)   (forty)

minutes, Kien was tired. He went to the ___*check-out lane*___ with a full cart.
                 (cashier's lane)

The ___*cashier*___ worked fast. Kien's bill was $43.16. Four
     (clerk)

___*sacks*___ of groceries! Kien decided not to forget his list next time!
    (bags)

Take Your Pick

This multiple choice exercise measures students' understanding of vocabulary meaning and usage in sentences.

Review the unit vocabulary using the pictures at the beginning of the unit. Explain any other new vocabulary in the exercise items before asking students to complete the exercise.

Tell the students to choose the word or phrase missing in each sentence from among the three choices listed under the sentence. Prefixes and suffixes that change word meaning appear in some of the answer choices. Have students write the missing word or phrase on the blank in each sentence.

Take Your Pick

There is a missing word or phrase in each sentence below. Read each sentence. Then, look at the three choices under the sentence. Choose the correct word or phrase and write it on the blank.

1. Angela _shops_ at Star Market once a week.

   shops   shopping   buys

2. The cereal is _on_ the top shelf.

   in   on   over

3. Mark needs two _quarts_ of milk.

   quarters   quarts   quart

4. They had a _sale_ at Michael's Grocery Store.

   sale   sell   sail

5. Tomas, what will you _buy_ at the sale?

   buy   by   bye

6. Do you have a _receipt_ ?

   buy   shopping   receipt

7. Cathy bought two _pounds_ of hamburger.

   boxes   pounds   cartons

8. The _canned_ foods are on aisle #3.

   shopping   canned   quart

9. Kim went _shopping_ after work.

   shop   shopping   shopped

10. The express lane _is_ fast.

    is   are   were

Bingo

1. Make the bingo cards.

Students create bingo cards through teacher dictation of vocabulary. The dictation provides a spelling assessment as well as a listening activity.

Instruct the students to look at the empty bingo grid in their book. The grid has nine squares for nine vocabulary items. Read the vocabulary to the class. Ask students to write the words in the boxes at random, not in rows. Each student should have a different bingo card after nine items are dictated.

2. Check students' spelling.

When the bingo cards are completed, write the vocabulary words on the board and ask students to check their spelling and make corrections.

3. Play bingo.

Distribute eight markers — such as paper clips, buttons, chips, or pennies — to each student. Read each oral cue twice in normal speech. Students find the corresponding vocabulary item on their cards and cover it with a marker. When one student has three in a row, he or she calls "bingo" and then reads off the words in the marked squares for checking. You may need to demonstrate how bingo is played for those students who have never played before.

There are two game options. Choose the one that best fits the students' level of proficiency, or use them both at different times of instruction.

Game 1

Vocabulary for Dictation	Teacher Cues
dairy	Milk, cheese, and cream.
bakery	Bread, rolls, and donuts.
deli	Sandwiches and salads.
produce	Lettuce, tomatoes, and carrots.
meat	Chicken, hamburger, and steak.
paper products	Napkins, Kleenex, and toilet paper.
frozen foods	Ice cream and pizza.
canned foods	Soup, peas, and pears.
beverages	Orange juice and soda.

Game 2

Vocabulary for Dictation	Teacher Cues
pound	Hamburger.
dozen	Eggs.
bottle	Soda pop and water.
box	Cereal.
quart	Milk.
sacks	Bags.
fast lane	Express lane.
can	Soup.
jar	Jelly.

Get It Together

The crossword puzzle provides practice in recognizing word meaning and usage.

Have students read each numbered clue and write the answer in the puzzle spaces with the same number. A word list of answers is given so that spelling will not hinder students' ability to complete the puzzle.

To quiz the spelling skills of more advanced students, ask the students to cover the word list while filling in the puzzle squares.

Get It Together

There is a word missing in each sentence below. Choose the correct word from the word list. Print that word in the boxes of the puzzle.

tomatoes	supermarket	frozen
bakery	list	dairy
lane	deli	sale
out	in	aisle

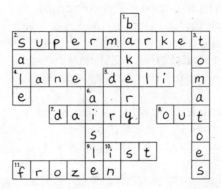

Across

2. Buy food at the _____ .

4. Only 7 items at the express _____ .

5. Buy sandwiches at the _____ .

7. Buy milk in the _____ section.

8. The sign on the exit says _____ .

9. Make a shopping _____ .

11. The _____ pizza is cold.

Down

1. Buy bread at the _____ .

2. There's a big _____ today.

3. The _____ are in the produce section.

6. The canned fruit is on _____ 3.

10. The sign on the entrance says _____ .

84 ◆ Unit 5

And There's More

1. Concentration

Copy and cut out individual pictures from the beginning of the unit. Mount the pictures on 3" x 5" cards. Label the back of the pictures with consecutive numbers. On an equal number of cards, write the names of the pictures. Then label the back of the cards with consecutive letters.

Lay all the cards on a large table, pictures and words facing down. Ask students to take turns choosing two cards, trying to match a picture with its word. Ask each student to read the word and identify the picture on the card he or she chooses. Then the student decides if the cards are a match. Check to be sure the student's decision is correct.

If there is no match, the cards are turned back over. If there is a match, the student keeps the pair of cards. The winner is the person who has the most matched cards.

Concentration helps exercise memory, gives review of letter and number names, and reinforces vocabulary.

2. Memory Circle

Have students sit in a circle and ask each to name an item that is purchased at a supermarket. You should start the dialogue by naming an item. The first student repeats the item you have named and adds another item. As the game continues, each student repeats what has been said, then adds a grocery item of his or her choice. Items may or may not be given in alphabetical order. Here's an example of how the activity should progress:

Teacher:	I have to go shopping. I need some apples.
First student:	I have to go shopping. I need some apples and bananas.
Second student:	I have to go shopping. I need some apples, bananas, and cucumbers.

In multilevel classes beginners should start the process and more advanced students should follow, so that the advanced students have to remember more items.

3. Guessing Game

Introduce adjectives that describe food shape, color, and taste. Real food can be used to enhance meaning. Use the words that follow:

red	hard	sweet	round
yellow	soft	sour	long
orange	big	salty	short
green	small		

Begin the game by describing a food item. Ask students to guess the name of the food. Here's an example:

Teacher:	I'm thinking of a food that is round, red, and sweet.
Student:	An apple.
Teacher:	No, it's small.
Student:	A cherry.
Teacher:	That's right.

After the game is demonstrated a few times, students take turns giving clues. Watch and facilitate the progress of the game. Let the students do all the talking.

The guessing game can exercise memory of food items and can provide practice with adjectives.

Unit 6

SHOPPING FOR CLOTHING

Picture It

The following pictures provide meaning for the life skills vocabulary used throughout the unit.

In this unit, the illustrations show many common clothing items, including a shirt, a coat, and a sweater. The illustrations also show parts of a department store and store personnel students may encounter when shopping for clothing. In addition, they provide examples of important information labels, such as a price tag and a care label.

Rather than introducing all vocabulary items before beginning the exercises, refer to the pictures while students complete the unit. If all the vocabulary is introduced before beginning the unit, students will have difficulty remembering meaning, pronunciation, and usage. Introduce the words in the context of the unit activities. For example, before asking students to complete "Guess Who, Where, or

What," use the pictures to show word meanings for the vocabulary in that exercise.

Pictures in the student's edition are not labeled. Learning meaning before seeing the written word facilitates comprehension and correct pronunciation. When introducing the vocabulary in the pictures, you may want to model each word and have the class repeat it after you. Give examples of the word in sentences. After meaning is clear and students can identify vocabulary items, they can label the pictures with your assistance. Once students have labeled the pictures, they can use this section to review word meaning and spelling.

Picture It

The following pictures show people and things that will be discussed in this unit. Refer to these pictures when doing exercises throughout the unit.

1. *women's clothing*   4. *sale sign*   7. *children's clothing*
2. *men's clothing*   5. *accessories*
3. *jewelry*   6. *shoes*

1. shirt and blouse

2. pants and shorts

3. coat and jacket

4. sweater

5. _pajamas and robe_

6. _night gown_

7. _dress_

9. _slip and underwear_

8. _suit_

10. _jewelry_

11. *belt and scarf*

12. *hat and gloves*

13. *shoes and socks*

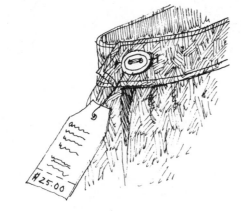

14. *price tag*

15. *care label*

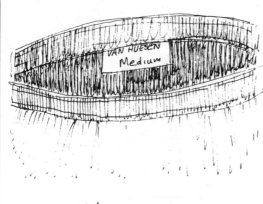

16. *medium*

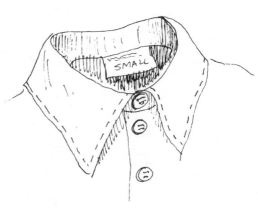

17. *small*

18. *fitting room*

19. *sales clerk*

20. *large*

21. *store manager*

22. *cashier*

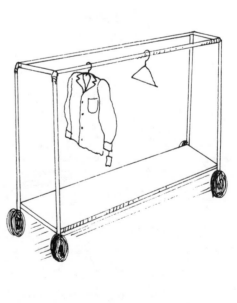

23. *clothes rack*

92 ◆ Unit 6

Give It a Try

This exercise provides practice of words in context.

After word meaning is introduced through pictures, read each group of phrases orally with the students' books closed. After the students master the phrases, they can open their books and read the phrases together.

You may need to explain words unfamiliar to the students before beginning the exercise. Begin the oral presentation by modeling each phrase. Have the students repeat the phrase. Then give a cue word. The students repeat the sentence with the new cue word.

Give It a Try

Practice the phrases listed below.

1. The _blouse_ is too small. Why don't you _exchange it_?

skirt	return it
shirt	take it back
sweater	give it back

2. I'd like that ___shirt___ in a size _15-1/2 by 34_.

belt	32
nightgown	6 or a small
hat	7-1/4
dress	12
jacket	38 regular

3. Where is the _women's clothing_ department? It's _straight ahead_.

men's clothing	on the third floor
jewelry	over there
accessories	in the basement
children's clothing	upstairs

4. He needs a new pair of __shoes__, but these are too _big_.

jeans	tight
pajamas	long
shorts	small
socks	large

5. How much is the _robe_? It's ___$17.99___.

jacket	$34.50
dress	$29.95 on sale
coat	$45.00
belt	$16.75 plus tax

6. The ___suits___ are in the _men's clothing_ section.

belts	accessories
necklaces	jewelry
bibs	children's clothing
blouses	women's clothing

Example:

Teacher: The blouse is too small. Why don't you exchange it?

Students: The blouse is too small. Why don't you exchange it?

Teacher: Skirt, return it.

Students: The skirt is too small. Why don't you return it?

Teacher: Shirt, take it back.

Students: The shirt is too small. Why don't you take it back?

Attention, Please!

This exercise provides practice in listening and reading.

Read each oral cue twice in normal speech. The cues are available only in the teacher's edition. Students listen to the cue, read the three choices in their books, and then circle the word or phrase identified by the cue. After the students complete the exercise, check their responses orally.

Attention, Please!

Listen to the teacher's cue. Then, circle the correct response.

1. aisle #2   (fitting room)   jewelry department

2. (jewelry)   coats   scarf

3. small   medium   (large)

4. (accessories)   jewelry   men's clothing

5. men's clothing   (women's clothing)   shoe department

6. sell   (exchange)   receipt

7. department   (cashier)   discount

8. (small)   medium   large

9. bag of shirts   (price of shirts)   rack of shirts

10. sell   give   (return)

11. (care label)   price tag   size

12. shoes   (sizes)   department

Teacher Cues

1. Try clothes on here.
2. Necklace, bracelet, and rings.
3. Big.
4. Gloves, scarves, and belts.
5. Blouse, dress, and skirt.
6. Return for a different size.
7. The person you pay.
8. Little.
9. Cost of shirts.
10. To take back.
11. Tells how to wash the clothes.
12. Small, medium, and large.

Tell Me About It

This is a pair activity. One student has information that another student needs, but doesn't have, in order to complete a task.

Divide the class into pairs of students. One person in each pair uses Part A; the other uses Part B. Parts A and B are back-to-back pages in the student's edition. Partners should be seated so that they can't see each other's pages. Partners take turns asking questions about items in the pictures. Referring to the visual clues and using directional words, students answer each other's questions and write the new information in the correct places on the pictures.

Monitor the activity by listening to each pair of students. After students complete all the questions, ask them to check their communication by comparing Parts A and B.

Tell Me About It (Part A)

Study the picture. Then, ask your partner the questions below. Using your partner's answers, write the name, price, and/or size of each underlined item in the correct place on the picture.

Where are the <u>hats</u>?
Where are the <u>sweaters</u>?
Where are the <u>shorts</u>?
Where are the <u>coats</u>?
Where are the <u>belts</u>?

How much are the <u>hats</u>?
How much are the <u>sweaters</u>?
How much are the <u>shorts</u>?
What's the <u>"Summer Special"</u>?

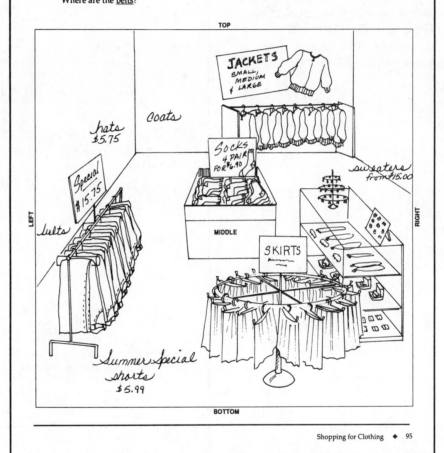

Tell Me About It (Part B)

Study the picture. Then, ask your partner the questions below. Using your partner's answers, write the name, price, and/or size of each underlined item in the correct place on the picture.

Where are the <u>pants</u>? How much are the <u>pants</u>?
Where are the <u>socks</u>? How much are the <u>socks</u>?
Where are the <u>jackets</u>? What sizes are the <u>jackets</u>?
Where is the <u>jewelry</u>? Where are the <u>skirts</u>?

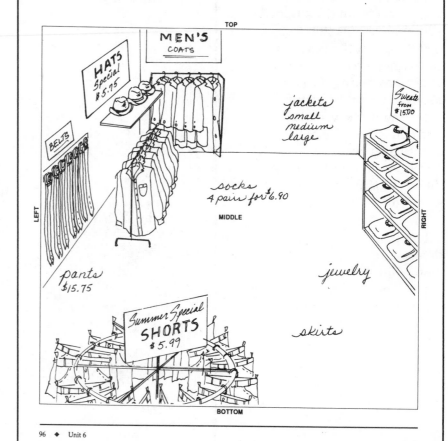

Guess Who, Where, or What

This is a category exercise that can be used with pairs of students in multilevel classes. It can also be completed by individual students. Having students list words under appropriate categories checks their understanding of word meanings.

Students read each word or phrase in the list and decide if it describes a person, place, or thing. Then each student writes the word or phrase in the correct category. You should categorize the first word to provide an example for the students.

Guess Who, Where, or What

Read each word or phrase in the list below. Ask a classmate if the word or phrase describes a person, place, or thing. Write the words in the correct category.

manager	hat	coat
children's clothing	jewelry department	clerk
tie	bracelet	scarf
dress	men's clothing department	accessories department
pants	customer	assistant manager
shoe department	cashier	sweater
fitting room	socks	women's clothing department
blouse		

People Seen at a Department Store	Places in a Department Store	Things to Buy in a Department Store
manager	shoe department	children's clothing
customer	fitting room	tie
cashier	jewelry department	dress
clerk	men's clothing department	pants
assistant manager	accessories department	blouse
	women's clothing department	hat
		bracelet
		socks
		coat
		scarf
		sweater

Two Against One

This category exercise checks students' understanding of word meaning and usage.

Explain the concept of a set to the class before beginning the exercise.

Ask students to read the three words in each set and then circle the word that doesn't belong to the set. Check the exercise orally by asking students to explain their choices. More than one answer is acceptable in some exercise sets. The students' explanation of their choices determines acceptable answers.

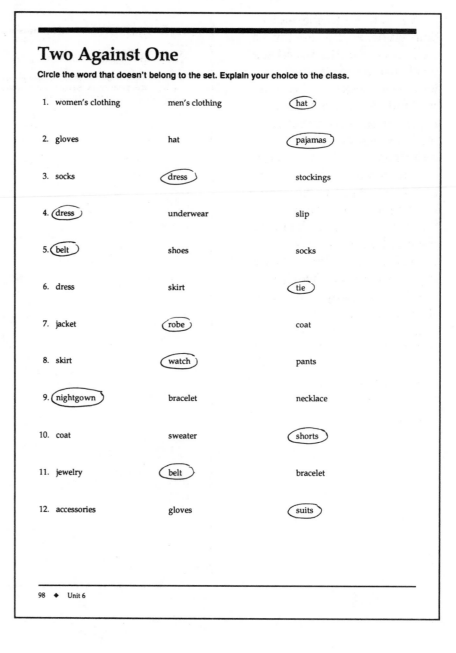

Two Against One

Circle the word that doesn't belong to the set. Explain your choice to the class.

1. women's clothing   men's clothing   (hat)

2. gloves   hat   (pajamas)

3. socks   (dress)   stockings

4. (dress)   underwear   slip

5. (belt)   shoes   socks

6. dress   skirt   (tie)

7. jacket   (robe)   coat

8. skirt   (watch)   pants

9. (nightgown)   bracelet   necklace

10. coat   sweater   (shorts)

11. jewelry   (belt)   bracelet

12. accessories   gloves   (suits)

Inside Story

This activity facilitates students' use of contextual clues and provides practice in finding synonyms. Rather than just measuring basic comprehension of vocabulary, the exercise fosters the skill of analysis.

First ask the students to read the entire story. Then ask them to find words from the word list that have the same meanings as the words under the blank lines in the story. Instruct the students to write the matching words on the blanks. You may want to fill in the first blank to provide the students with an example. When all the matching words are found and all the blanks are filled in, students should read the story again using the new words.

Inside Story

Read the story below. Choose words or phrases from the list that have the same meanings as the words or phrases under the lines. Write the correct words on the blanks. Read the story again using the words written on the blanks.

little	jeans	eight
big	discount	start
$12.00	right	fast
department	sales	ad
children's	racks	

Rena's Shopping Trip

Rena's daughter, Joanna, is _____eight_____ years old. She is growing
(8)

_____fast_____ . Joanna is going back to school in September, and she needs some
(quickly)

new clothes.

Rena decided to go to Brown's _____discount_____ store for the back-to-school
(low cost)

_____sales_____ . She saw an _____ad_____ in the weekend
(bargains)   (advertisement)

paper. Everything was on sale!

The _____children's_____ clothing _____department_____ was crowded.
(young people's)   (section)

The _____jeans_____ were only $9.50. The sweaters were
(denim pants)

_____$12.00_____ . There were two _____racks_____ of skirts on
(twelve dollars)   (bars)

sale. Rena didn't know where to _____start_____ .
(begin)

Rena held up a sweater. Is this too _____big_____ ? Rena held up a skirt. Is
(large)

this too _____little_____ ? It was hard to guess the _____right_____ size.
(small)   (correct)

Rena had to bring Joanna back to the store to try on the clothes.

Take Your Pick

This multiple choice exercise measures students' understanding of vocabulary meaning and usage in sentences.

Review the unit vocabulary using the pictures at the beginning of the unit. Explain any other new vocabulary in the exercise items before asking students to complete the exercise.

Tell the students to choose the word or phrase missing in each sentence from among the three choices listed under the sentence. Prefixes and suffixes that change word meaning appear in some of the answer choices. Have students write the missing word or phrase on the blank in each sentence.

Take Your Pick

There is a missing word or phrase in each sentence below. Read each sentence. Then, look at the three choices under the sentence. Choose the correct word or phrase and write it on the blank.

1. The shirts _were_ on sale yesterday.

   was   is   were

2. The blouses are _on_ sale today.

   in   on   under

3. John is looking for the men's _clothing department_.

   cloth department   clothings department   clothing department

4. He wore his new _pajamas_ last night.

   pajamas   pajama   pajama's

5. Carlos needed to _try on_ the suit.

   try in   try out   try on

6. Where is the _jewelry_ department?

   jewels   jewelry   jewelries

7. Karim is in the _fitting_ room.

   fitting   fit   fitted

8. Molly wants to _exchange_ the sweater. It's too big.

   change   exchange   fitting

9. The blouse is _too_ big.

   to   too   two

10. Sein needs a sweater to _match_ the pants.

    match   matches   matching

Bingo

1. Make the bingo cards.

Students create bingo cards through teacher dictation of vocabulary. The dictation provides a spelling assessment as well as a listening activity.

Instruct the students to look at the empty bingo grid in their book. The grid has nine squares for nine vocabulary items. Read the vocabulary to the class. Ask students to write the words in the boxes at random, not in rows. Each student should have a different bingo card after nine items are dictated.

2. Check students' spelling.

When the bingo cards are completed, write the vocabulary words on the board and ask students to check their spelling and make corrections.

3. Play bingo.

Distribute eight markers — such as paper clips, buttons, chips, or pennies — to each student. Read each oral cue twice in normal speech. Students find the corresponding vocabulary item on their cards and cover it with a marker. When one student has three in a row, he or she calls "bingo" and then reads off the words in the marked squares for checking. You may need to demonstrate how bingo is played for those students who have never played before.

There are two game options. Choose the one that best fits the students' level of proficiency, or use them both at different times of instruction.

Game 1

Vocabulary for Dictation	Teacher Cues
hat	Wear this on top of your head.
gloves	Wear these on your hands.
coat	Wear this over your clothes on cold days.
slip	Wear this under a dress.
shoes	Wear these on your feet.
belt	Wear this around your waist.
pajamas	Wear these for sleeping.
scarf	Wear this around your neck.
bracelet	Wear this on your wrist.

Game 2

Vocabulary for Dictation	Teacher Cues
cashier	You pay him at the store.
care label	It tells how to wash the shirt.
fitting room	A place to try on clothes.
jewelry	Bracelet, ring, and earrings.
customer	She buys clothes.
receipt	A list of costs.
sale	Bargains.
size	Small, medium, or large.
return	To take something back.

Get It Together

The crossword puzzle provides practice in recognizing word meaning and usage.

Have students read each numbered clue and write the answer in the puzzle spaces with the same number. A word list of answers is given so that spelling will not hinder students' ability to complete the puzzle.

To quiz the spelling skills of more advanced students, ask the students to cover the word list while filling in the puzzle squares.

Get It Together

There is a word missing in each sentence below. Choose the correct word from the word list. Print that word in the boxes of the puzzle.

ad	large	pants
suit	tie	aisles
medium	sales	shirt
shopping	department	men
small	need	

Across

2. The _____ is in the newspaper.

3. Buy clothes at a _____ store.

6. Take a _____ list to the store.

9. He wore a _____ and tie.

10. The shirts on aisle 2 are for _____ , not women.

12. The dress is tight. It's too _____ .

13. The _____ is size 12.

Down

1. The hat is very big. It's size _____ .

2. The children's clothing section is on _____ 3 and 4.

4. The shirt is not large or small. It's _____ .

5. He wore a coat and _____ .

7. He wore a pair of _____ .

8. The store has many _____ today.

11. You _____ some new clothes.

And There's More

1. Concentration

Copy and cut out individual pictures from the beginning of the unit. Mount the pictures on 3" x 5" cards. Label the back of the pictures with consecutive numbers. On an equal number of cards, write the names of the pictures. Then label the back of the cards with consecutive letters.

Lay all the cards on a large table, pictures and words facing down. Ask students to take turns choosing two cards, trying to match a picture with its word. Ask each student to read the word and identify the picture on the card he or she chooses. Then the student decides if the cards are a match. Check to be sure the student's decision is correct.

If there is no match, the cards are turned back over. If there is a match, the student keeps the pair of cards. The winner is the person who has the most matched cards.

Concentration helps exercise memory, gives review of letter and number names, and reinforces vocabulary.

2. Memory Circle

Have students sit in a circle and ask each to name a clothing item that will be packed for a long trip. You should start the dialogue by naming an item. The first student repeats the item you have named and adds another item. As the game continues, each student repeats what has been said, then adds an item of clothing of his or her choice. Items may or may not be given in alphabetical order. Here's an example of how the activity should progress:

Teacher:	She's going on vacation. She needs to pack a blouse.
First student:	She's going on vacation. She needs to pack a blouse and a coat.
Second student:	She's going on vacation. She needs to pack a blouse, a coat, and a dress.

In multilevel classes beginners should start the process and more advanced students should follow, so that the advanced students have to remember more items.

3. Role Play

Bring several items of clothing to class, such as the following:

shirt	sweater
skirt	dress
socks	pair of pants
blouse	pair of shoes
pair of shorts	

Each item should have a size label. Pin a mock price tag to each item.

Ask students to role play the following situations:

- returning an item (possible reasons — size, color, style, etc. are unsuitable)
- exchanging an item (possible reasons — size, color, style, etc. are unsuitable)
- buying clothes on sale (asking about sale price, savings, etc.)
- asking to try on an item

During role play note the students' language proficiency. Rather than correct errors during the role play, note the errors and use them for future lessons.

Unit 7

TRANSPORTATION

Picture It

The following pictures provide meaning for the life skills vocabulary used throughout the unit.

The illustrations in this unit show different modes of transportation. The illustrations also include transportation workers and places to go for transportation such as a bus station or airport. In addition, a view of a service station illustrates a scene with a customer and an attendant pumping gas, a cashier at a register, a mechanic working on a car, and a car entering a carwash. The interior and exterior of a car are also shown so that students can learn the vocabulary necessary to communicate with service personnel.

Rather than introducing all vocabulary items before beginning the exercises, refer to the pictures while students complete the unit. If all the vocabulary is introduced before beginning the unit, students will have difficulty remembering meaning, pronunciation, and usage. Introduce the words in the context of the unit activities. For example, before asking students to complete "Guess Who, Where, or What," use the pictures to show word meanings for the vocabulary in that exercise.

Pictures in the student's edition are not labeled. Learning meaning before seeing the written word facilitates comprehension and correct pronunciation. When introducing the vocabulary in the pictures, you may want to model each word and have the class repeat it after you. Give examples of the word in sentences. After meaning is clear and students can identify vocabulary items, they can label the pictures with your assistance. Once students have labeled the pictures, they can use this section to review word meaning and spelling.

Picture It

The following pictures show people and things that will be discussed in this unit. Refer to these pictures when doing exercises throughout the unit.

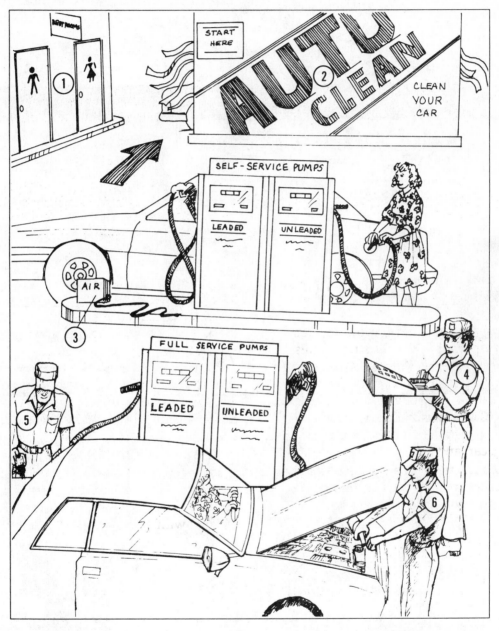

1. *restrooms*
2. *carwash*
3. *air hose*
4. *cashier*
5. *station attendant*
6. *mechanic*

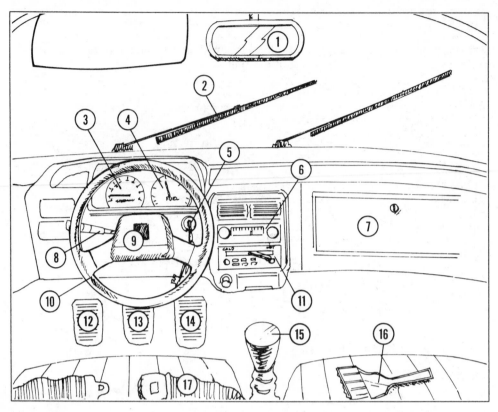

1. rear view mirror
2. windshield wiper
3. speedometer
4. gas gauge
5. ignition
6. radio
7. glove box
8. turn signal
9. horn
10. steering wheel
11. heater
12. clutch
13. brake
14. gas pedal
15. gear shift
16. scraper
17. seatbelt

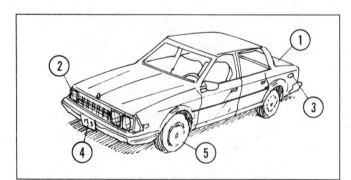

1. trunk
2. lights
3. gas tank
4. license plate
5. tire

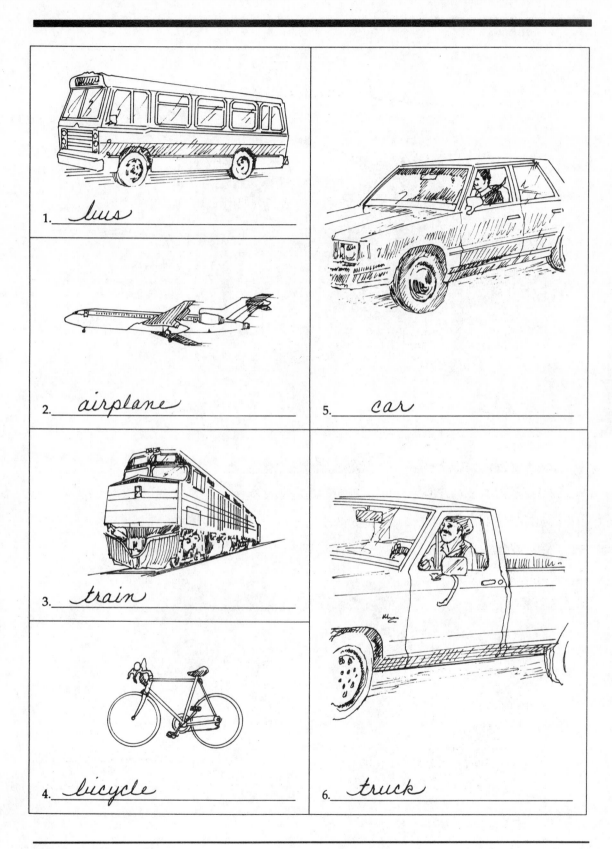

1. bus

2. airplane

3. train

4. bicycle

5. car

6. truck

7. _taxi_

8. _bus driver_

9. _pilot_

10. _flight attendant_

11. _bus station_

12. _airport_

Give It a Try

This exercise provides practice of words in context.

After word meaning is introduced through pictures, read each group of phrases orally with the students' books closed. After the students master the phrases, they can open their books and read the phrases together.

You may need to explain words unfamiliar to the students before beginning the exercise. Begin the oral presentation by modeling each phrase. Have the students repeat the phrase. Then give a cue word. The students repeat the sentence with the new cue word.

Give It a Try

Practice the phrases listed below.

1. Would you check the __oil__ , please? _____Certainly_____ .

tires	Of course.
battery	I'd be glad to.
brakes	What's the problem?
clutch	I'm sorry, I can't right now.

2. Did the mechanic fix the _speedometer_ ? _Yes, she did_ .

brakes	
ignition	
gear shift	No, she didn't

3. The _gas gauge_ isn't working. The _____brakes_____ aren't working.

   | turn signal | lights |
   | radio | windshield wipers |

4. There's a _mechanic_ on duty, isn't there? Yes, there is.

   | bus driver |
   | taxi driver |

5. I need a gas station with a _self service pump_ .

   | carwash |
   | garage |
   | restroom |

6. Is the _taxi_ late? _Yes, it's thirty minutes late_ .

bus	
plane	
train	No, it's early

7. Where's the _garage_ ? In the _____main square_____ .

map	glove compartment
jack	trunk
car	garage

8. He uses _____regular gas_____ in the _truck_ .

   | unleaded gas | taxi |
   | diesel fuel | bus |

Example:

Teacher: Would you check the oil, please? Certainly.

Students: Would you check the oil, please? Certainly.

Teacher: Tires, of course.

Students: Would you check the tires, please? Of course.

Teacher: Battery, I'd be glad to.

Students: Would you check the battery, please? I'd be glad to.

Attention, Please!

This exercise provides practice in listening and reading.

Before asking students to complete the exercise, introduce terms such as *roll down*, *open*, *turn*, *close*, *push*, and *fill*. Introduce these terms with actions, mime, or visual aids.

Read each oral cue twice in normal speech. The cues are available only in the teacher's edition. Students listen to the cue, read the three choices in their books, and then circle the word or phrase identified by the cue. After the students complete the exercise, check their responses orally.

Attention, Please!

Listen to the teacher's cue. Then, circle the correct response.

1. (steering wheel)   brake   gas pedal

2. tires   (trunk)   key

3. (glove compartment) radio   ignition

4. radio   glove compartment (clutch)

5. (brakes)   key   gear shift

6. speedometer   (key)   gas gauge

7. (ignition)   radio   gear shift

8. gas gauge   trunk   (window)

9. (battery)   radio   lights

10. (gas tank)   speedometer   seatbelt

11. brakes   (seatbelt)   trunk

12. (horn)   tires   key

Teacher Cues

1. Turn it.
2. Open it.
3. Close it.
4. Push it in.
5. Step on them.
6. Turn it.
7. Put the key into it.
8. Roll it down.
9. Check it.
10. Fill it.
11. Fasten it.
12. Blow it.

Tell Me About It

This is a pair activity. One student has information that another student needs, but doesn't have, in order to complete a task.

Divide the class into pairs of students. One person in each pair uses Part A; the other uses Part B. Parts A and B are back-to-back pages in the student's edition. Partners should be seated so that they can't see each other's pages. Partners take turns asking questions about items in the pictures. Referring to the visual clues and using directional words, students answer each other's questions and write the new information in the correct places on the pictures.

Monitor the activity by listening to each pair of students. After students complete all the questions, ask them to check their communication by comparing Parts A and B.

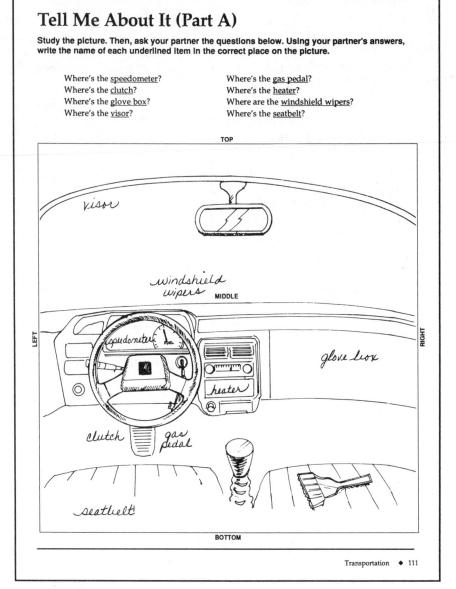

Tell Me About It (Part A)

Study the picture. Then, ask your partner the questions below. Using your partner's answers, write the name of each underlined item in the correct place on the picture.

Where's the <u>speedometer</u>?
Where's the <u>clutch</u>?
Where's the <u>glove box</u>?
Where's the <u>visor</u>?

Where's the <u>gas pedal</u>?
Where's the <u>heater</u>?
Where are the <u>windshield wipers</u>?
Where's the <u>seatbelt</u>?

TOP

LEFT

RIGHT

visor

windshield wipers MIDDLE

speedometer

glove box

heater

clutch   *gas pedal*

seatbelt

BOTTOM

Transportation ◆ 111

Tell Me About It (Part B)

Study the picture. Then, ask your partner the questions below. Using your partner's answers, write the name of each underlined item in the correct place on the picture.

Where's the radio?
Where's the rear view mirror?
Where are the lights?
Where's the brake?

Where's the turn signal?
Where's the gas gauge?
Where's the ignition?

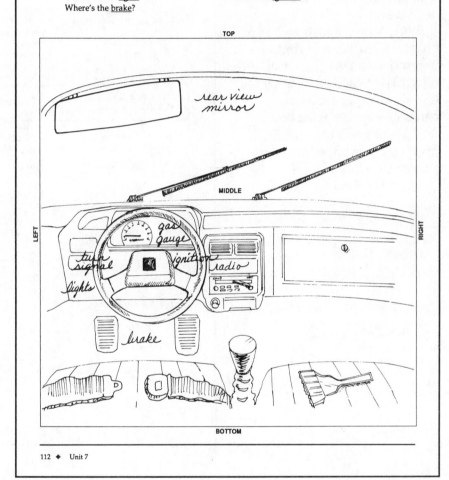

112 ◆ Unit 7

Guess Who, Where, or What

This is a category exercise that can be used with pairs of students in multilevel classes. It can also be completed by individual students. Having students list words under appropriate categories checks their understanding of word meanings.

Students read each word or phrase in the list and decide if it describes a person, place, or thing. Then each student writes the word or phrase in the correct category. You should categorize the first word to provide an example for the students.

Guess Who, Where, or What

Read each word or phrase in the list below. Ask a classmate if the word or phrase describes a person, place, or thing. Write the words in the correct category.

bus driver	bus station	steering wheel
airport	gear shift	pilot
cab driver	train station	glove box
mechanic	garage	speedometer
gas gauge	station attendant	carwash
visor	truck driver	seatbelt
flight attendant	bus stop	ignition
police officer	gas pedal	turn signal

People Who Work in Transportation	Transportation Places	Things Inside a Car
bus driver	airport	gas gauge
cab driver	bus station	visor
mechanic	train station	gear shift
flight attendant	garage	gas pedal
police officer	bus stop	steering wheel
station attendant	carwash	glove box
truck driver		speedometer
pilot		seat belt
		ignition
		turn signal

Two Against One

This category exercise checks students' understanding of word meaning and usage.

Explain the concept of a set to the class before beginning the exercise.

Ask students to read the three words in each set and then circle the word that doesn't belong to the set. Check the exercise orally by asking students to explain their choices. More than one answer is acceptable in some exercise sets. The students' explanation of their choices determines acceptable answers.

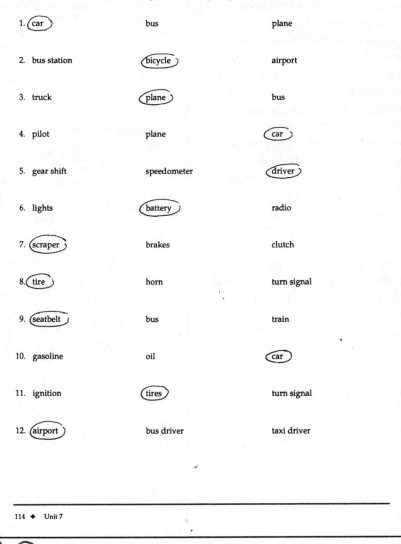

Two Against One

Circle the word that doesn't belong to the set. Explain your choice to the class.

1. (car)   bus   plane

2. bus station   (bicycle)   airport

3. truck   (plane)   bus

4. pilot   plane   (car)

5. gear shift   speedometer   (driver)

6. lights   (battery)   radio

7. (scraper)   brakes   clutch

8. (tire)   horn   turn signal

9. (seatbelt)   bus   train

10. gasoline   oil   (car)

11. ignition   (tires)   turn signal

12. (airport)   bus driver   taxi driver

Not a good exercise too many ways to look at it.

Inside Story

This activity facilitates students' use of contextual clues and provides practice in finding synonyms. Rather than just measuring basic comprehension of vocabulary, the exercise fosters the skill of analysis.

First ask the students to read the entire story. Then ask them to find words from the word list that have the same meanings as the words under the blank lines in the story. Instruct the students to write the matching words on the blanks. You may want to fill in the first blank to provide the students with an example. When all the matching words are found and all the blanks are filled in, students should read the story again using the new words.

Inside Story

Read the story below. Choose words or phrases from the list that have the same meanings as the words or phrases under the lines. Write the correct words on the blanks. Read the story again using the words written on the blanks.

battery	service station	driver's seat
horn	lights	got out of
gas pedal	ignition	clutch
dashboard	radio	start
windshield	seatbelt	scraper
morning		

A Cold Morning for Juan

It was a very cold December _morning_ (A.M.) . Juan used his

scraper (cleaner) to clean the ice from his _windshield_ (front car window) . He got

into the _driver's seat_ (seat behind the wheel) , fastened the _seatbelt_ (belt) , and put

the key into the _ignition_ (starter) .

The lights on the _dashboard_ (panel) were red, but the car didn't

start (turn on) . Juan put in the _clutch_ (pedal on the left) and stepped on

the _gas pedal_ (pedal on the right) . He turned the key again. Nothing. Only a rumble.

Now what? Juan tried the _lights_ (lamps) . They didn't work. Juan tried the

horn (honker) . It didn't work. Juan tried the _radio_ (music player) .

It didn't work.

"The _battery_ (electric current box) ! It's too old. It's too cold," he exclaimed. Juan

got out of (exited) the car and called a _service station_ (gas station) .

Transportation ◆ 115

Take Your Pick

This multiple choice exercise measures students' understanding of vocabulary meaning and usage in sentences.

Review the unit vocabulary using the pictures at the beginning of the unit. Explain any other new vocabulary in the exercise items before asking students to complete the exercise.

Tell the students to choose the word or phrase missing in each sentence from among the three choices listed under the sentence. Prefixes and suffixes that change word meaning appear in some of the answer choices. Have students write the missing word or phrase on the blank in each sentence.

Take Your Pick

There is a missing word or phrase in each sentence below. Read each sentence. Then, look at the three choices under the sentence. Choose the correct word or phrase and write it on the blank.

1. Juan missed the bus, so he took a _taxi_ to work.
   taxi   ticket   pilot

2. The flight was _cancelled_ , so Margarita couldn't go at all.
   late   early   cancelled

3. The _airport_ was so crowded, Maria missed her flight.
   airport   bus station   train station

4. The _bus driver_ missed the turn on 5th Street.
   pilot   attendant   bus driver

5. She got a ticket because she was _driving_ without a license.
   flying   driving   drive

6. Margo took her car to the _garage_ to be fixed.
   garage   carwash   airport

7. When Juanita passed the test, she got her _driver's license_ .
   driver's license   traffic license   mother's license

8. Mario borrowed Juan's _truck_ to move his heavy furniture.
   bicycle   train   truck

9. Step on the _brakes_ !
   speedometer   brakes   ignition

10. Don't forget to fasten your _seatbelt_ .
    seatbelt   steering wheel   windows

Bingo

1. Make the bingo cards.

Students create bingo cards through teacher dictation of vocabulary. The dictation provides a spelling assessment as well as a listening activity.

Instruct the students to look at the empty bingo grid in their book. The grid has nine squares for nine vocabulary items. Read the vocabulary to the class. Ask students to write the words in the boxes at random, not in rows. Each student should have a different bingo card after nine items are dictated.

2. Check students' spelling.

When the bingo cards are completed, write the vocabulary words on the board and ask students to check their spelling and make corrections.

3. Play bingo.

Distribute eight markers — such as paper clips, buttons, chips, or pennies — to each student. Read each oral cue twice in normal speech. Students find the corresponding vocabulary item on their cards and cover it with a marker. When one student has three in a row, he or she calls "bingo" and then reads off the words in the marked squares for checking. You may need to demonstrate how bingo is played for those students who have never played before.

There are two game options. Choose the one that best fits the students' level of proficiency, or use them both at different times of instruction.

Game 1

Vocabulary for Dictation	Teacher Cues
mechanic	I fixed the speedometer.
bus driver	Please use the exact change.
police officer	Can I see your license?
pilot	We are flying at 30,000 feet.
taxi driver	Where to?
gas station attendant	Shall I check the oil?
cashier	That's nine dollars and fifty-five cents.
passenger	Where can I sit?
flight attendant	Coffee or soda?

Game 2

Vocabulary for Dictation	Teacher Cues
speedometer	Fifty-five miles per hour.
direction signal	Left or right turn.
gear shift	First, second, third, or fourth.
scraper	For cleaning the windshield.
gas gauge	Full or empty.
seatbelt	Fasten this.
brakes	For stopping.
glove box	The map is inside.
trunk	The spare tire is inside.

Get It Together

The crossword puzzle provides practice in recognizing word meaning and usage.

Have students read each numbered clue and write the answer in the puzzle spaces with the same number. A word list of answers is given so that spelling will not hinder students' ability to complete the puzzle.

To quiz the spelling skills of more advanced students, ask the students to cover the word list while filling in the puzzle squares.

Get It Together

There is a word missing in each sentence below. Choose the correct word from the word list. Print that word in the boxes of the puzzle.

seatbelt	restroom	speedometer	can
cashier	horn	gas	mechanic
full	wash	license	radio
pedal	key		

Puzzle solution (filled in):

Row 1: s p e e d o m e t e r
Across 1 (s-p-e-e-d-o-m-e-t-e-r), with 2. down "pedal", 3. down "mechanic", 4. down "restroom"

- 1. speedometer
- 5. radio
- 6. gas
- 7. full
- 8. license
- 9. wash
- 10. horn
- 11. cashier
- 12. can
- 13. key
- 14. seatbelt
- 2. pedal
- 3. mechanic
- 4. restroom

Across

1. The _____ reads 65 mph.

5. The _____ plays music.

6. The gauge says "E." I need _____ .

7. The gauge says "F." It means _____ .

11. Pay the _____ .

12. Put the paper in the trash _____ .

14. Fasten your _____ .

Down

2. Step on the gas _____ .

3. The _____ fixes cars.

4. He's in the men's _____ .

8. I need to see your registration and your

   driver's _____ .

9. The car is dirty. Go to the car _____ .

10. Honk the _____ .

13. Put the _____ in the ignition.

And There's More

1. Concentration

Copy and cut out individual pictures from the beginning of the unit. Mount the pictures on 3" x 5" cards. Label the back of the pictures with consecutive numbers. On an equal number of cards, write the names of the pictures. Then label the back of the cards with consecutive letters.

Lay all the cards on a large table, pictures and words facing down. Ask students to take turns choosing two cards, trying to match a picture with its word. Ask each student to read the word and identify the picture on the card he or she chooses. Then the student decides if the cards are a match. Check to be sure the student's decision is correct.

If there is no match, the cards are turned back over. If there is a match, the student keeps the pair of cards. The winner is the person who has the most matched cards.

Concentration helps exercise memory, gives review of letter and number names, and reinforces vocabulary.

2. The Car of Your Dreams

Have each student cut out a picture of a car from a magazine. Each student should paste his or her picture on an 8 1/2" x 11" piece of paper and write a description of the car underneath the picture. The student must try to sell the car by describing its best features. Here are some possible feature descriptions:

4-door	Stereo!
New!	4 new tires
Big trunk!	35 m.p.g.
Red seatbelts!	Room for eight

Students can present their pages to other class members and tell about their cars.

3. Write an Ad

Ask students to write a newspaper ad to sell their own car or an imaginary one. Introduce these abbreviations before assigning the task:

4 dr.	4 doors
2 dr.	2 doors
low mi.	low mileage
exc. cond.	excellent condition
auto.	automatic
w/	with
'78	1978
AC	air conditioning
pwr.	power
eng.	engine
4 spd.	4 speed
syst.	system

Have students include the following information in the ad:

- description of car
- car year
- price
- phone number and times to call

4. Sign Tic-Tac-Toe

Prepare a grid as shown below on the board or overhead transparency. Divide the class into two teams, Team *X* and Team *O*. Each team member has a chance to choose a sign, give the sign name, and tell what the sign means. If the person answers correctly, his or her team gets an *X* or *O* in that square. If the person answers incorrectly, the turn is lost. A team wins when there are three *X*'s or *O*'s in a row.

Make additional signs for another grid. The signs in the following list can be made with no words for cues. Sign shape and figures or arrows convey meaning.

no left turn	do not enter
no right turn	road construction
men working	25 m.p.h.
side road	intersection
deer crossing	

Tic-tac-toe grids can also be made by copying the pictures at the beginning of the unit and pasting each one on a grid square. The students get an *X* or *O* by naming a vocabulary item and using it correctly in a sentence.

Unit 8

COMMUNITY SERVICES

Picture It

The following pictures provide meaning for the life skills vocabulary used throughout the unit.

People who work in community services are illustrated in this unit. Examples of service personnel depicted are a librarian, a fire fighter, and a doctor. Also presented are two community maps with labeled streets and different buildings where community services are offered. Students can use these maps for practice in giving directions and for identifying buildings.

Rather than introducing all vocabulary items before beginning the exercises, refer to the pictures while students complete the unit. If all the vocabulary is introduced before beginning the unit, students will have difficulty remembering meaning, pronunciation, and usage. Introduce the words in the context of the unit activities. For example, before asking students to complete "Guess Who, Where, or

What," use the pictures to show word meanings for the vocabulary in that exercise.

Pictures in the student's edition are not labeled. Learning meaning before seeing the written word facilitates comprehension and correct pronunciation. When introducing the vocabulary in the pictures, you may want to model each word and have the class repeat it after you. Give examples of the word in sentences. After meaning is clear and students can identify vocabulary items, they can label the pictures with your assistance. Once students have labeled the pictures, they can use this section to review word meaning and spelling.

Picture It

The following pictures show people and things that will be discussed in this unit. Refer to these pictures when doing exercises throughout the unit.

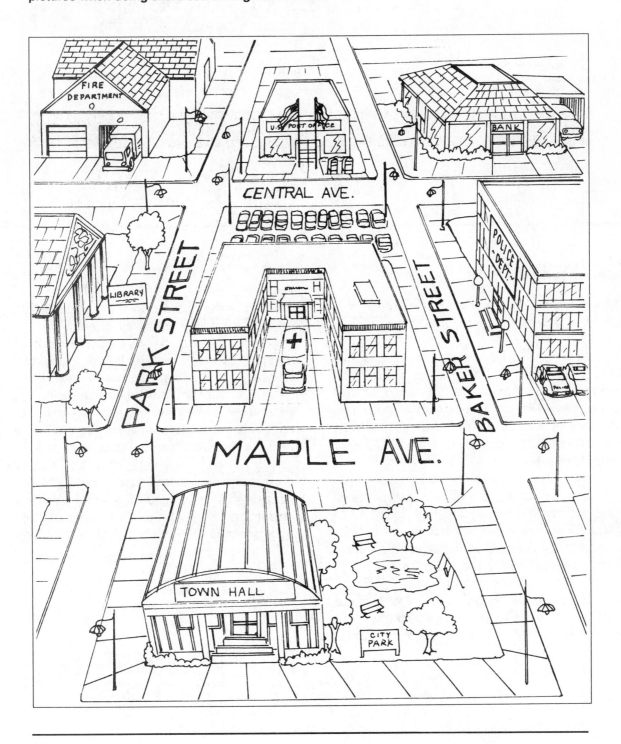

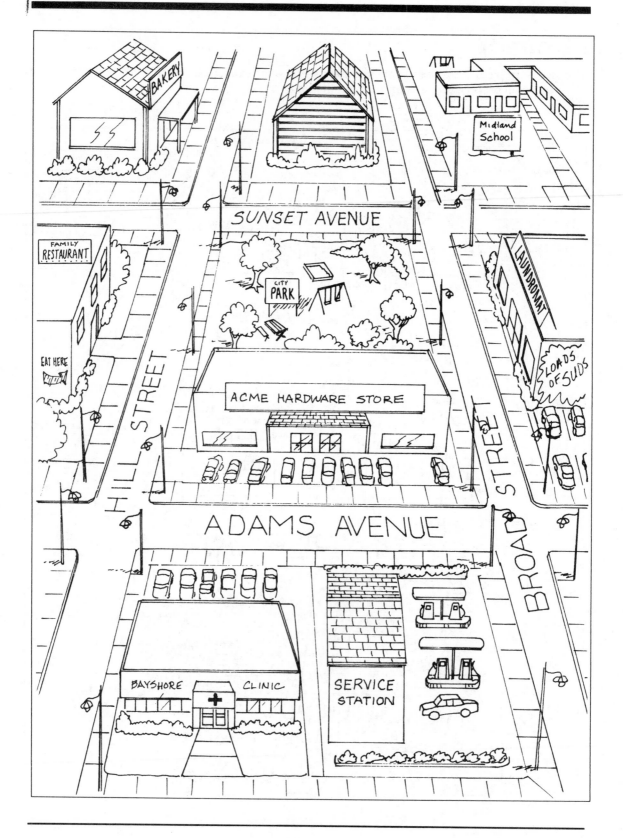

1. *bank teller*

2. *baker*

3. *clerk*

4. *librarian*

5. _teacher_

6. _doctor_

7. _waitress_

8. _police officer_

9. *fire fighter*

10. *mail carrier*

11. *cashier*

12. *service station attendant*

Give It a Try

This exercise provides practice of words in context.

After word meaning is introduced through pictures, read each group of phrases orally with the students' books closed. After the students master the phrases, they can open their books and read the phrases together.

You may need to explain words unfamiliar to the students before beginning the exercise. Begin the oral presentation by modeling each phrase. Have the students repeat the phrase. Then give a cue word. The students repeat the sentence with the new cue word.

Give It a Try

Practice the phrases listed below.

1. The ___bank___ is closed on Sunday.
   post office
   clinic
   town hall

2. The ___bakery___ is open on Sunday.
   service station
   library
   laundromat
   hospital

3. Where is the _police department_?
   fire department
   service station
   hardware store

4. The ___school___ is on the corner of 5th Street and Baker Street.
   laundromat
   restaurant
   post office

5. The _librarian_ works at the ___library___ until 4:00 P.M.
   teller   bank
   cashier   hardware store
   doctor   clinic

6. _Police officers_ work on Sunday.
   Waiters
   Librarians
   Fire fighters

7. The _service station attendant_ takes your money.
   cashier
   store clerk
   teller

Example:

Teacher: The bank is closed on Sunday.

Students: The bank is closed on Sunday.

Teacher: Post office.

Students: The post office is closed on Sunday.

Teacher: Clinic.

Students: The clinic is closed on Sunday.

Attention, Please!

This exercise provides practice in listening and reading.

Read each oral cue twice in normal speech. The cues are available only in the teacher's edition. Students listen to the cue, read the three choices in their books, and then circle the word or phrase identified by the cue. After the students complete the exercise, check their responses orally.

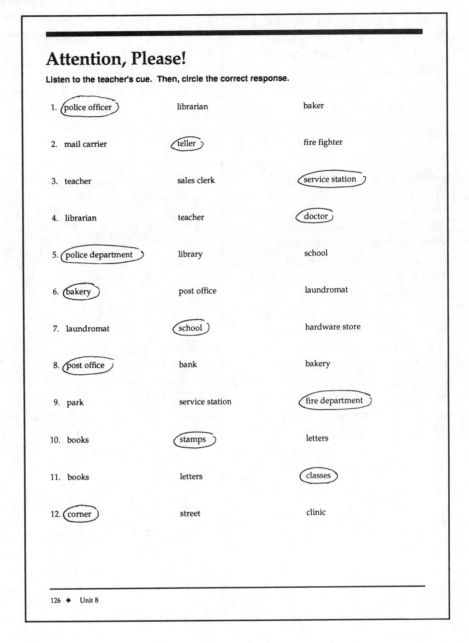

Attention, Please!

Listen to the teacher's cue. Then, circle the correct response.

1. (police officer)   librarian   baker

2. mail carrier   (teller)   fire fighter

3. teacher   sales clerk   (service station)

4. librarian   teacher   (doctor)

5. (police department)   library   school

6. (bakery)   post office   laundromat

7. laundromat   (school)   hardware store

8. (post office)   bank   bakery

9. park   service station   (fire department)

10. books   (stamps)   letters

11. books   letters   (classes)

12. (corner)   street   clinic

126 ◆ Unit 8

Teacher Cues

1. She works at the police department.
2. She works at the bank.
3. Go there for gasoline.
4. He works at the clinic.
5. Go there for an accident report.
6. Go there to buy bread.
7. A principal works there.
8. Mail a letter there.
9. Report an emergency there.
10. Buy these at the post office.
11. Take these at school.
12. Place where two streets meet.

Tell Me About It

This is a pair activity. One student has information that another student needs, but doesn't have, in order to complete a task.

Divide the class into pairs of students. One person in each pair uses Part A; the other uses Part B. Parts A and B are back-to-back pages in the student's edition. Partners should be seated so that they can't see each other's pages. Partners take turns asking questions about items in the pictures. Referring to the visual clues and using directional words, students answer each other's questions and write the new information in the correct places on the pictures.

Monitor the activity by listening to each pair of students. After students complete all the questions, ask them to check their communication by comparing Parts A and B.

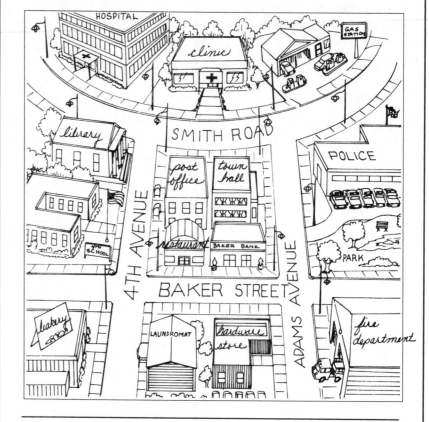

Tell Me About It (Part A)

Study the picture. Then, ask your partner the questions below. Using your partner's answers, write the name of each underlined item in the correct place on the picture.

Where's the <u>hardware store</u>?　　Where's the <u>town hall</u>?
Where's the <u>library</u>?　　Where's the <u>fire department</u>?
Where's the <u>clinic</u>?　　Where's the <u>post office</u>?
Where's the <u>restaurant</u>?　　Where's the <u>bakery</u>?

Tell Me About It (Part B)

Study the picture. Then, ask your partner the questions below. Using your partner's answers, write the name of each underlined item in the correct place on the picture.

Where's the <u>school</u>?
Where's the <u>hospital</u>?
Where's the <u>laundromat</u>?
Where's the <u>bank</u>?

Where's the <u>park</u>?
Where's the <u>police department</u>?
Where's the <u>service station</u>?

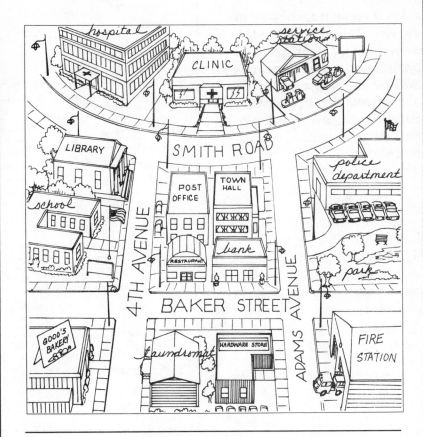

Guess Who, Where, or What

This is a category exercise that can be used with pairs of students in multilevel classes. It can also be completed by individual students. Having students list words under appropriate categories checks their understanding of word meanings.

Students read each word or phrase in the list and decide if it describes a person, place, or thing. Then each student writes the word or phrase in the correct category. You should categorize the first word to provide an example for the students.

Guess Who, Where, or What

Read each word or phrase in the list below. Ask a classmate if the word or phrase describes a person, place, or thing. Write the words in the correct category.

teller	bank	
post office	park	service station
X-ray	gasoline	cashier
doctor	hospital	library
town hall	waitress	fire department
books	deposit	physical exam
clinic	accident report	breakfast
nurse	police officer	librarian
stamps	mail carrier	hammer and nails

People Working in Community Services	Community Services	Services Provided
teller	post office	X-ray
doctor	town hall	books
nurse	clinic	stamps
waitress	bank	gasoline
police officer	park	deposit
mail carrier	hospital	accident report
cashier	service station	physical exam
librarian	library	breakfast
	fire department	hammer and nails

Two Against One

This category exercise checks students' understanding of word meaning and usage.

Explain the concept of a set to the class before beginning the exercise.

Ask students to read the three words in each set and then circle the word that doesn't belong to the set. Check the exercise orally by asking students to explain their choices. More than one answer is acceptable in some exercise sets. The students' explanation of their choices determines acceptable answers.

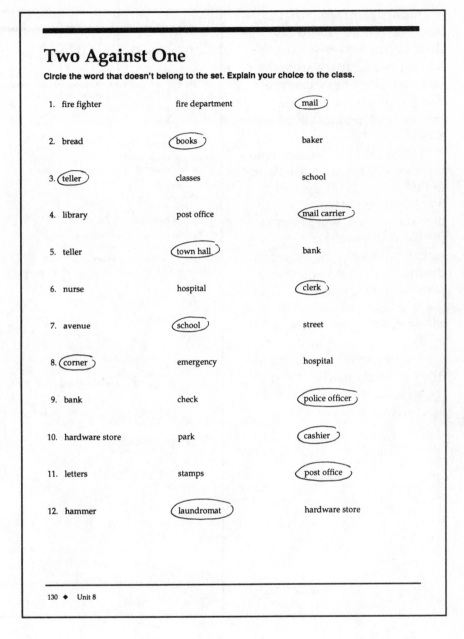

Two Against One

Circle the word that doesn't belong to the set. Explain your choice to the class.

1. fire fighter   fire department   (mail)

2. bread   (books)   baker

3. (teller)   classes   school

4. library   post office   (mail carrier)

5. teller   (town hall)   bank

6. nurse   hospital   (clerk)

7. avenue   (school)   street

8. (corner)   emergency   hospital

9. bank   check   (police officer)

10. hardware store   park   (cashier)

11. letters   stamps   (post office)

12. hammer   (laundromat)   hardware store

Inside Story

This activity facilitates students' use of contextual clues and provides practice in finding synonyms. Rather than just measuring basic comprehension of vocabulary, the exercise fosters the skill of analysis.

First ask the students to read the entire story. Then ask them to find words from the word list that have the same meanings as the words under the blank lines in the story. Instruct the students to write the matching words on the blanks. You may want to fill in the first blank to provide the students with an example. When all the matching words are found and all the blanks are filled in, students should read the story again using the new words.

Inside Story

Read the story below. Choose words or phrases from the list that have the same meanings as the words or phrases under the lines. Write the correct words on the blanks. Read the story again using the words written on the blanks.

buy	make a deposit	2:30
clinic	return	service station
police department	tired	Then
errands to run	mail	Tuesday
an appointment	books	clothes

Kim's Errands

Kim had many _errands to run_ on _Tuesday_. She had
                   (places to go)   (Tues.)

to go to the post office to _buy_ stamps and
                               (purchase)

mail a package. _Then_, she had to go to the
  (send)   (After that)

bank to _make a deposit_. Then, to the library to _return_
    (put money into her account)   (take back)

some _books_. Then, to the _clinic_. Her son,
     (reading material)   (health-care facility)

Kien, had _an appointment_ at _2:30_.
        (a visit time)   (two-thirty)

She also had to fill her car at the _service station_, wash a load of
                              (gas station)

clothes at the laundromat, and buy a bike license at the
  (laundry)

police department.
 (police station)

What a busy day! She was _tired_ just thinking about it!
               (exhausted)

Take Your Pick

This multiple choice exercise measures students' understanding of vocabulary meaning and usage in sentences.

Review the unit vocabulary using the pictures at the beginning of the unit. Explain any other new vocabulary in the exercise items before asking students to complete the exercise.

Tell the students to choose the word or phrase missing in each sentence from among the three choices listed under the sentence. Prefixes and suffixes that change word meaning appear in some of the answer choices. Have students write the missing word or phrase on the blank in each sentence.

Take Your Pick

There is a missing word or phrase in each sentence below. Read each sentence. Then, look at the three choices under the sentence. Choose the correct word or phrase and write it on the blank.

1. The *baker* works at the bakery.

   baker   bake   bread

2. A mail carrier *delivers* mail to your house.

   delivery   delivers   deliver

3. The *teller* cashes checks at the bank.

   teller   tell   told

4. Jose went to the *police department* for an accident report.

   department police   police   police department

5. I want to *check out* this book.

   check out   check around   check over

6. Where *is* the laundromat?

   are   were   is

7. What time does the library *close* ?

   close   closed   closing

8. The police *officer* stopped the car.

   office   department   officer

9. The park is *on* the corner of 5th Street and James Avenue.

   in   over   on

10. Farid went to the service station to *fill* his car with gas.

    fill   full   filled

Bingo

1. Make the bingo cards.

Students create bingo cards through teacher dictation of vocabulary. The dictation provides a spelling assessment as well as a listening activity.

Instruct the students to look at the empty bingo grid in their book. The grid has nine squares for nine vocabulary items. Read the vocabulary to the class. Ask students to write the words in the boxes at random, not in rows. Each student should have a different bingo card after nine items are dictated.

2. Check students' spelling.

When the bingo cards are completed, write the vocabulary words on the board and ask students to check their spelling and make corrections.

3. Play bingo.

Distribute eight markers — such as paper clips, buttons, chips, or pennies — to each student. Read each oral cue twice in normal speech. Students find the corresponding vocabulary item on their cards and cover it with a marker. When one student has three in a row, he or she calls "bingo" and then reads off the words in the marked squares for checking. You may need to demonstrate how bingo is played for those students who have never played before.

There are two game options. Choose the one that best fits the students' level of proficiency, or use them both at different times of instruction.

Game 1

Vocabulary for Dictation	Teacher Cues
post office	I need twenty stamps, please.
library	I want to check out this book.
bank	I want to make a withdrawal.
police department	I need to report an accident.
bakery	I need two loaves of bread, please.
clinic	I have an appointment with Doctor Jones.
restaurant	I'd like a cup of coffee and a roll, please.
hardware store	I need a hammer.
school	I want to take an English class.

Game 2

Vocabulary for Dictation	Teacher Cues
post office	Buy stamps here.
library	Borrow books here.
police department	Get a bike license here.
bakery	Buy bread here.
restaurant	Go out to dinner here.
clinic	Get a physical exam here.
avenue	Another name for *street*.
school	Take an English class here.
park	Have a picnic here.

Get It Together

The crossword puzzle provides practice in recognizing word meaning and usage.

Have students read each numbered clue and write the answer in the puzzle spaces with the same number. A word list of answers is given so that spelling will not hinder students' ability to complete the puzzle.

To quiz the spelling skills of more advanced students, ask the students to cover the word list while filling in the puzzle squares.

Get It Together

There is a word missing in each sentence below. Choose the correct word from the word list. Print that word in the boxes of the puzzle.

restaurant	park	library	laundromat
clinic	avenue	corner	fire
school	bank	service	out
bakery			

Across

1. He takes English classes at _____ .

4. Eat lunch at the _____ .

5. Call the _____ department for emergencies.

7. The bank is on the _____ of 5th and Hill St.

9. The abbreviation for _____ is ave.

10. They had a picnic in the _____ .

11. Return the books to the _____ .

Down

1. Buy gasoline at the _____ station.

2. They're going _____ for lunch.

3. Wash clothes at the _____ .

6. He made a deposit at the _____ .

7. He has an appointment at the _____ .

8. Buy bread at the _____ .

And There's More

1. Charades

Write each job listed below on a 3" x 5" card:

police officer	fire fighter
librarian	mail carrier
doctor	nurse
waitress	service station
teacher	banker
store clerk	baker

One student volunteers to give non-verbal clues to the class. The student chooses one of the cards and mimes the job duties. The other students try to guess the job title. For example, a student can act out the duties of a doctor by pretending to use a stethoscope to listen to someone's heart or by pretending to look into someone's ear or throat.

When the job title is guessed, another student chooses a card and continues the game. The game continues until all the cards have been chosen.

2. Who Said That?

Before beginning this exercise with the students, review the community services introduced at the beginning of the unit. Then read one of the cues that follow. Students guess where the sentence may have been said and who may have said it. Here's an example:

Teacher: Take a deep breath.
Student: A doctor or nurse says that in a clinic or hospital.

Teacher cues:

1. Take a deep breath.
2. Shall I check the oil?
3. Open your books to page two.
4. There's postage due on this package.
5. I need to see your license, please.
6. In a fire, get out of the house quickly.
7. The bread is fresh today.
8. The children's books are downstairs.
9. May I take your order?

3. Tic-Tac-Toe

Prepare a grid as shown below on the board or overhead transparency. An alternate grid can be prepared by copying the pictures at the beginning of the unit and pasting each one on a grid square.

1. police officer	2. fire fighter	3. waitress
4. baker	5. teller	6. service station attendant
7. teacher	8. nurse	9. librarian

Divide the class into two teams, Team X and Team O. Each team member has a chance to choose a square, identify the person in the square, and tell where he or she works. If the person answers correctly, his or her team gets an X or O in that square. If the person answers incorrectly, the turn is lost. A team wins when there are three X's or O's in a row. Here's an example of how you might proceed:

Teacher: Choose a square and answer the questions: Who is it? and Where does he or she work?
Student: I choose square number two. The fire fighter works at the fire department.
Teacher: Correct. You get an X.

Picture It

The following pictures provide meaning for the life skills vocabulary used throughout the unit.

In this unit, the illustrations show people and locations within a bank. The pictures also show the most common bills and coins used in the United States. In addition, they provide examples of important banking forms and cards, such as a deposit slip, a bank statement, and an ATM card.

Rather than introducing all vocabulary items before beginning the exercises, refer to the pictures while students complete the unit. If all the vocabulary is introduced before beginning the unit, students will have difficulty remembering meaning, pronunciation, and usage. Introduce the words in the context of the unit activities. For example, before asking students to complete "Guess Who, Where, or What," use the pictures to show word meanings for the vocabulary in that exercise.

Pictures in the student's edition are not labeled. Learning meaning before seeing the written word facilitates comprehension and correct pronunciation. When introducing the vocabulary in the pictures, you may want to model each word and have the class repeat it after you. Give examples of the word in sentences. After meaning is clear and students can identify vocabulary items, they can label the pictures with your assistance. Once students have labeled the pictures, they can use this section to review word meaning and spelling.

Picture It

The following pictures show people and things that will be discussed in this unit. Refer to these pictures when doing exercises throughout the unit.

1. *teller*
2. *safe*
3. *bank manager*
4. *receptionist*

1. _ATM_

2. _drive-up window_

3. _teller_

4. _reception desk_

5. *bank president*

6. *security guard*

7. *safe*

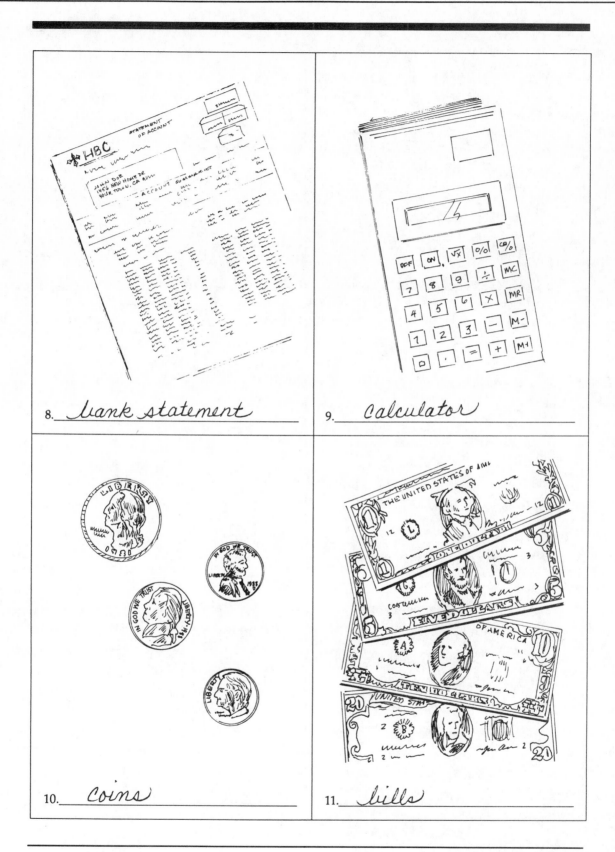

8. _bank statement_

9. _calculator_

10. _coins_

11. _bills_

12. *deposit slip and receipt*

13. *checkbook*

14. *check*

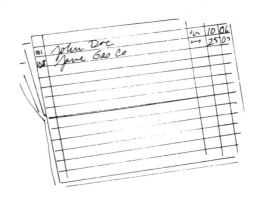

15. *check register*

16. *ATM card*

17. *credit card*

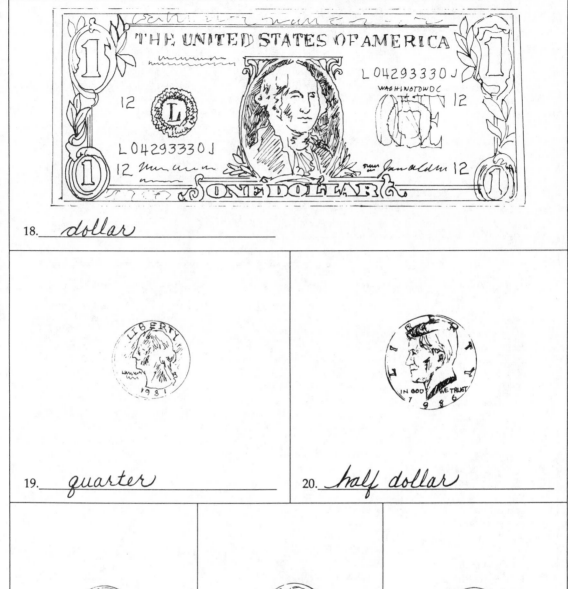

18. _dollar_

19. _quarter_

20. _half dollar_

21. _penny_

22. _nickel_

23. _dime_

24. *five dollar bill*

25. *ten dollar bill*

26. *twenty dollar bill*

Give It a Try

This exercise provides practice of words in context.

After word meaning is introduced through pictures, read each group of phrases orally with the students' books closed. After the students master the phrases, they can open their books and read the phrases together.

You may need to explain words unfamiliar to the students before beginning the exercise. Begin the oral presentation by modeling each phrase. Have the students repeat the phrase. Then give a cue word. The students repeat the sentence with the new cue word.

Give It a Try

Practice the phrases listed below.

1. He wrote a check for __$50.00__.
   - $25.00
   - $42.00
   - $12.00
   - $15.00

2. She filled out the __deposit slip__.
   - check register
   - bank statement
   - receipt

3. Add the amounts on the __calculator__.
   - deposit slip
   - check register
   - bank statement
   - receipt

4. Do you have change for __$1.00__?
   - $5.00
   - $10.00
   - a quarter
   - $20.00

5. Pay the bill with __a check__.
   - a credit card
   - cash
   - bills

6. Don't go inside. Use the __drive-up window__.
   - automatic-teller machine
   - night deposit box

7. I lost my __checkbook__.
   - ATM card
   - credit card
   - change

Example:

Teacher: Pay the bill with a check.

Students: Pay the bill with a check.

Teacher: A credit card.

Students: Pay the bill with a credit card.

Teacher: Cash.

Students: Pay the bill with cash.

Attention, Please!

This exercise provides practice in listening and reading.

Read each oral cue twice in normal speech. The cues are available only in the teacher's edition. Students listen to the cue, read the three choices in their books, and then circle the word or phrase identified by the cue. After the students complete the exercise, check their responses orally.

Attention, Please!

Listen to the teacher's cue. Then, circle the correct response.

1.	penny	(nickel)	dime
2.	(quarter)	half dollar	penny
3.	($5.75)	$5.57	$5.65
4.	($15.15)	$50.15	$15.50
5.	(coins)	bills	checks
6.	check register	withdrawal	(deposit)
7.	(bank statement)	bank teller	bank account
8.	coins	(bills)	tellers
9.	(credit card)	bank card	note card
10.	charge	check	(cash)
11.	25¢	$1.00	(10¢)
12.	(drive-up window)	teller	checkbook

Teacher Cues

1. Five cents.
2. Twenty-five cents.
3. Five seventy-five.
4. Fifteen dollars and fifteen cents.
5. Pennies, nickels, and dimes.
6. Put money in the bank.
7. Record of checks, deposits, and withdrawals.
8. A five dollar bill and a ten dollar bill.
9. Use this to charge it.
10. Coins and bills.
11. Dime.
12. Place to do banking outside.

Tell Me About It

This is a pair activity. One student has information that another student needs, but doesn't have, in order to complete a task.

Divide the class into pairs of students. One person in each pair uses Part A; the other uses Part B. Parts A and B are back-to-back pages in the student's edition. Partners should be seated so that they can't see each other's pages. Partners take turns asking questions about items in the pictures. Referring to the visual clues and using directional words, students answer each other's questions and write the new information in the correct places on the pictures.

Monitor the activity by listening to each pair of students. After students complete all the questions, ask them to check their communication by comparing Parts A and B.

Tell Me About It (Part A)

Study the check. Then, ask your partner the questions below. Fill in the check using your partner's answers.

What's the check number?	Who is the check to?
What's the Matas' address?	What's the account number?

Jose or Maria Mata
621 Smith Street
San Diego, CA 92128

1809

Date March 1 19 89

Pay to the order of Mr. Carlos García $ 350.00

Three Hundred Fifty xx/100   Dollars

South Bank of San Diego

For rent   Signature Maria Mata

78/89765-001

Study the deposit slip. Then, ask your partner the questions below. Fill in the deposit slip using your partner's answers.

What's the date?	What's the name of the bank?
How many checks are deposited?	How much is each check for?

For Deposit to the Account of

Jose or Maria Mata
621 Smith Street
San Diego, CA 92128

Date April 30 19 89

Signature José Mata

South Bank of San Diego

78/89765-001

	CURRENCY		
CASH	COIN		
CHECKS	1	420	50
	2	70	00
	3		
	4		
TOTAL		490	50
LESS CASH RECEIVED		90	50
NET DEPOSIT		400	00

Tell Me About It (Part B)

Study the check. Then, ask your partner the questions below. Fill in the check using your partner's answers.

What's the date?   How much is the check for?
What's the money for?   Who is writing the check?

Jose or Maria Mata 621 Smith Street San Diego, CA 92128	1809 Date _March 1_ 19 _89_

Pay to the order of _Mr. Carlos Garcia_ $ _350.00_

Three Hundred Fifty ⁰⁰/₁₀₀ ————————— Dollars

⬣ **South Bank**
  of San Diego

For _rent_   Signature _Maria Mata_

78/89765-001

Study the deposit slip. Then, ask your partner the questions below. Fill in the deposit slip using your partner's answers.

Who is making the deposit?   What's the account number?
What's the total of checks deposited?   How much cash is received?
What's the total deposit?

For Deposit to the Account of

Jose or Maria Mata
621 Smith Street
San Diego, CA 92128

Date _April 30_   19 _89_

Signature _José Mata_

⬣ **South Bank**
  of San Diego

78/89765-001

CASH	CURRENCY		
	COIN		
CHECKS	1	420	50
	2	70	00
	3		
	4		
TOTAL		490	50
LESS CASH RECEIVED		90	50
NET DEPOSIT		400	00

Guess Who, Where, or What

This is a category exercise that can be used with pairs of students in multilevel classes. It can also be completed by individual students. Having students list words under appropriate categories checks their understanding of word meanings.

Students read each word or phrase in the list and decide if it describes a person, place, or thing. Then each student writes the word or phrase in the correct category. You should categorize the first word to provide an example for the students.

Guess Who, Where, or What

Read each word or phrase in the list below. Ask a classmate if the word or phrase describes a person, place, or thing. Write the words in the correct category.

teller	bank manager	safe
coins	drive-up window	security guard
checkbook	receptionist	banker
office	bank	deposit
customer	check register	bills
automatic-teller machine	information desk	bank statement
check	deposit slip	calculator

People in the Bank	Places for Banking	Things in Banking
teller	office	coins
customer	automatic-teller machine	checkbook
bank manager	drive-up window	check
receptionist	bank	check register
security guard	information desk	deposit slip
banker		safe
		deposit
		bills
		bank statement
		calculator

Two Against One

This category exercise checks students' understanding of word meaning and usage.

Explain the concept of a set to the class before beginning the exercise.

Ask students to read the three words in each set and then circle the word that doesn't belong to the set. Check the exercise orally by asking students to explain their choices. More than one answer is acceptable in some exercise sets. The students' explanation of their choices determines acceptable answers.

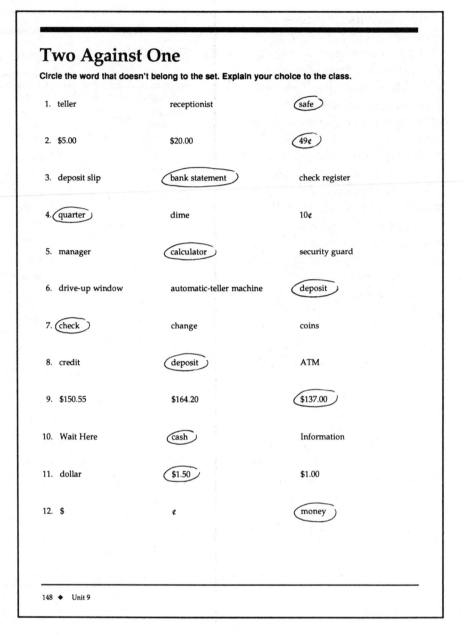

Two Against One

Circle the word that doesn't belong to the set. Explain your choice to the class.

1. teller   receptionist   (safe)

2. $5.00 $20.00   (49¢)

3. deposit slip   (bank statement)   check register

4. (quarter)   dime   10¢

5. manager   (calculator)   security guard

6. drive-up window   automatic-teller machine   (deposit)

7. (check)   change   coins

8. credit   (deposit)   ATM

9. $150.55 $164.20   ($137.00)

10. Wait Here   (cash)   Information

11. dollar   ($1.50) $1.00

12. $ ¢   (money)

Inside Story

This activity facilitates students' use of contextual clues and provides practice in finding synonyms. Rather than just measuring basic comprehension of vocabulary, the exercise fosters the skill of analysis.

First ask the students to read the entire story. Then ask them to find words from the word list that have the same meanings as the words under the blank lines in the story. Instruct the students to write the matching words on the blanks. You may want to fill in the first blank to provide the students with an example. When all the matching words are found and all the blanks are filled in, students should read the story again using the new words.

Inside Story

Read the story below. Choose words or phrases from the list that have the same meanings as the words or phrases under the lines. Write the correct words on the blanks. Read the story again using the words written on the blanks.

credit card	$29.00	total
cash	charge	write
checkbook	$15.00	Friday
purse	store	prices
$20.50		

Campan's Shopping Trip

Campan went shopping for some new clothes on ____Friday____ . She picked
                                                  (Fri.)

out a new dress for ____$29.00____ , a pair of pants for
                     (twenty-nine dollars)

____$15.00____ , and a pair of shoes for ____$20.50____ .
    (fifteen dollars)   (twenty dollars and fifty cents)

The clerk added the ____prices____ and said, "That
                        (costs)

____total____ is $68.50 with tax. Cash or ____charge____ ?"
    (final amount)   (put on account)

Campan said she wanted to ____write____ a check. She took her
                              (make out)

____checkbook____ out of her ____purse____ . "Oh, no!" she said, "I
    (book of checks)   (bag)

used my last check at the other ____store____ ."
                                    (shop)

The clerk said Campan could use a ____credit card____ . Campan didn't have a
                                      (charge card)

credit card, so she had to pay with ____cash____ . She decided it was time to go
                                        (bills and coins)

home.

Take Your Pick

This multiple choice exercise measures students' understanding of vocabulary meaning and usage in sentences.

Review the unit vocabulary using the pictures at the beginning of the unit. Explain any other new vocabulary in the exercise items before asking students to complete the exercise.

Tell the students to choose the word or phrase missing in each sentence from among the three choices listed under the sentence. Prefixes and suffixes that change word meaning appear in some of the answer choices. Have students write the missing word or phrase on the blank in each sentence.

Take Your Pick

There is a missing word or phrase in each sentence below. Read each sentence. Then, look at the three choices under the sentence. Choose the correct word or phrase and write it on the blank.

1. Waldek wrote a _check_ to pay the telephone bill.

   checking   check   checks

2. Do you have _change_ for $20.00?

   change   changing   changes

3. Saul filled out the deposit _slip_ .

   sleep   ship   slip

4. Wait _here_ , please.

   here   hear   where

5. Raul used his _calculator_ to total the bill.

   calculation   calculating   calculator

6. They keep money in a _safe_ .

   save   savings   safe

7. Where is the _security guard_ ?

   security guard   guard security   secure guard

8. Kim used her _credit card_ for I.D.

   ATM check   ATM card   credit card

9. If you don't have much time, go to the _drive-up window_ .

   drive-up window   drive-in window   drive-around window

10. I have to _cash a check_ .

   change a check   check a cash   cash a check

Bingo

1. Make the bingo cards.

Students create bingo cards through teacher dictation of vocabulary. The dictation provides a spelling assessment as well as a listening activity.

Instruct the students to look at the empty bingo grid in their book. The grid has nine squares for nine vocabulary items. Read the vocabulary to the class. Ask students to write the words in the boxes at random, not in rows. Each student should have a different bingo card after nine items are dictated.

2. Check students' spelling.

When the bingo cards are completed, write the vocabulary words on the board and ask students to check their spelling and make corrections.

3. Play bingo.

Distribute eight markers — such as paper clips, buttons, chips, or pennies — to each student. Read each oral cue twice in normal speech. Students find the corresponding vocabulary item on their cards and cover it with a marker. When one student has three in a row, he or she calls "bingo" and then reads off the words in the marked squares for checking. You may need to demonstrate how bingo is played for those students who have never played before.

There are two game options. Choose the one that best fits the students' level of proficiency, or use them both at different times of instruction.

Game 1

Vocabulary for Dictation	Teacher Cues
six dollars and six cents	Six-oh-six.
fourteen dollars and eighty-eight cents	Fourteen eighty-eight.
forty-seven dollars and fifteen cents	Forty-seven fifteen.
twenty dollars and ninety-four cents	Twenty ninety-four.
penny	One cent.
quarter	Twenty-five cents.
half dollar	Fifty cents.
forty-seven dollars and fifty cents	Forty-seven fifty.
two dollars and ninety-four cents	Two ninety-four.

Game 2

Vocabulary for Dictation	Teacher Cues
teller	Takes money at the bank.
check register	Record of checks.
credit card	Charge card.
bills	One dollar, five dollars, ten dollars and twenty dollars.
coins	Penny, nickel, dime, and quarter.
deposit	Put money into the bank.
security guard	Keeps the bank safe.
calculator	Adding machine.
wait here	A sign at the bank.

Get It Together

The crossword puzzle provides practice in recognizing word meaning and usage.

Have students read each numbered clue and write the answer in the puzzle spaces with the same number. A word list of answers is given so that spelling will not hinder students' ability to complete the puzzle.

To quiz the spelling skills of more advanced students, ask the students to cover the word list while filling in the puzzle squares.

Get It Together

There is a word missing in each sentence below. Choose the correct word from the word list. Print that word in the boxes of the puzzle.

account	dime	bank	dollar
check	calculator	coin	penny
wait	up	register	three
two	nickels		

Across

2. Add the amounts on your pocket _____ .

6. I have to write a _____ .

10. One dime is two _____ .

11. A nickel is a _____ .

12. The word for 3 is _____ .

13. _____ here, please.

Down

1. The security guard works at the _____ .

3. She wants to open a checking _____ .

4. Go to the drive-_____ window.

5. Add and subtract in the check _____ .

7. Ten cents is a _____ .

8. One cent is a _____ .

9. One _____ is 100 pennies.

14. The word for 2 is _____ .

And There's More

1. Strip Sentences

Write each of the words in the following sentences on a separate 3" x 5" card. Mix up the cards for each sentence. Ask students to put the cards for each sentence in order. Punctuation marks and capital letters can be used as clues.

Do you have change for a dollar?

He wrote a check for $50.00.

Pay the bill with a credit card.

Don't go inside; use the drive-up window.

She filled out a deposit slip.

The teller works on Saturdays.

I lost my ATM card.

2. Relay Race

Divide the students into two teams, Team *A* and Team *B*. Ask one player from each team to go to the board. Dictate a number and have the students write the dictated number on the board. The first student to finish writing the number correctly gets a point. Each team player gets a chance to try for a point. The team with the most points wins the game.

Ask the students to write the numbers in words or in digits, depending on class level and proficiency. Here are some sample numbers to dictate:

forty-five

fifty-four

five hundred and fifty-four

four hundred and fifty-four

fifty-five dollars

fifty-four dollars and forty-five cents

fifteen

fifty

five hundred

five hundred and forty-five dollars and ninety cents

six hundred and seventy-eight dollars and thirty-two cents

Picture It

The following pictures provide meaning for the life skills vocabulary used throughout the unit.

The illustrations in this unit show several hotel-related jobs. The illustrations also show locations within and around the hotel. They present examples of important employment forms and information students may encounter or need to recognize when pursuing or beginning employment.

Rather than introducing all vocabulary items before beginning the exercises, refer to the pictures while students complete the unit. If all the vocabulary is introduced before beginning the unit, students will have difficulty remembering meaning, pronunciation, and usage. Introduce the words in the context of the unit activities. For example, before asking students to complete "Guess Who, Where, or What," use the pictures to show word meanings for the vocabulary in that exercise.

Pictures in the student's edition are not labeled. Learning meaning before seeing the written word facilitates comprehension and correct pronunciation. When introducing the vocabulary in the pictures, you may want to model each word and have the class repeat it after you. Give examples of the word in sentences. After meaning is clear and students can identify vocabulary items, they can label the pictures with your assistance. Once students have labeled the pictures, they can use this section to review word meaning and spelling.

Picture It

The following pictures show people and things that will be discussed in this unit. Refer to these pictures when doing exercises throughout the unit.

1. _desk clerk_
2. _hotel manager_
3. _operator_
4. _custodian_
5. _lobby_
6. _receptionist_
7. _bellhop_

1. _taxi driver_   2. _taxi_   3. _groundskeeper_

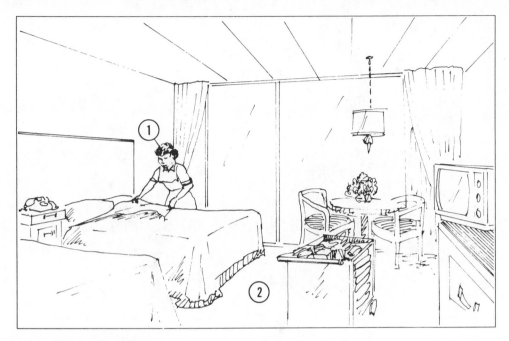

1. _housekeeper_   2. _guest room_

1. _waitress_   3. _waiter_

2. _cook_   4. _busboy_

1. _personnel office_

2. _job interview_

Employment ◆ 157

3. *want ads*

4. *full-time*

5. *part-time*

6. *paycheck*

7. *time card*

8. *job application*

9. *benefits*

Give It a Try

This exercise provides practice of words in context.

After word meaning is introduced through pictures, read each group of phrases orally with the students' books closed. After the students master the phrases, they can open their books and read the phrases together.

You may need to explain words unfamiliar to the students before beginning the exercise. Begin the oral presentation by modeling each phrase. Have the students repeat the phrase. Then give a cue word. The students repeat the sentence with the new cue word.

Give It a Try

Practice the phrases listed below.

1. The _waitress_ works part time at the restaurant.
   waiter
   cook
   hostess

2. The _housekeeper_ cleans after 2:00 P.M.
   custodian
   busboy
   groundskeeper

3. If you have a question, ask the _receptionist_.
   clerk
   manager
   bellhop

4. The manager tells about the ___benefits___.
   wages
   time card
   job application

5. The _taxi driver_ meets the guests.
   bellhop
   receptionist

6. The _secretary_ answers the phone.
   operator
   receptionist

7. Do you want _full-time work_?
   part-time work
   an interview
   a job application

8. I need to ask about ___benefits___.
   wages
   paychecks
   the want ad

Example:

Teacher: The secretary answers the phone.

Students: The secretary answers the phone.

Teacher: Operator.

Students: The operator answers the phone.

Teacher: Receptionist.

Students: The receptionist answers the phone.

Attention, Please!

This exercise provides practice in listening and reading.

Read each oral cue twice in normal speech. The cues are available only in the teacher's edition. Students listen to the cue, read the three choices in their books, and then circle the word or phrase identified by the cue. After the students complete the exercise, check their responses orally.

Attention, Please!

Listen to the teacher's cue. Then, circle the correct response.

1. hostess — (desk clerk) — groundskeeper
2. (cashier) — custodian — operator
3. taxi driver — (housekeeper) — groundskeeper
4. desk clerk — security guard — (waitress)
5. (bellhop) — waiter — cook
6. secretary — (hostess) — housekeeper
7. (taxi driver) — custodian — cook
8. waiter — groundskeeper — (manager)
9. (custodian) — taxi driver — waitress
10. receptionist — (groundskeeper) — desk clerk
11. (busboy) — security guard — secretary
12. (secretary) — custodian — groundskeeper

160 ◆ Unit 10

Teacher Cues

1. Here's your key to room two-oh-seven.
2. Your bill is forty-two dollars and fifty cents.
3. I'll clean room two-oh-eight at two o'clock.
4. May I take your order?
5. I can help you with your luggage.
6. How many for dinner?
7. I can take you to the airport in twenty minutes.
8. The hotel employee meeting is at seven-thirty in my office.
9. I clean the lobby.
10. I need to water the lawn.
11. I'll clean those tables now.
12. I'll type the letters.

Tell Me About It

This is a pair activity. One student has information that another student needs, but doesn't have, in order to complete a task.

Divide the class into pairs of students. One person in each pair uses Part A; the other uses Part B. Parts A and B are back-to-back pages in the student's edition. Partners should be seated so that they can't see each other's pages. Partners take turns asking questions about items in the pictures. Referring to the visual clues and using directional words, students answer each other's questions and write the new information in the correct places on the pictures.

Monitor the activity by listening to each pair of students. After students complete all the questions, ask them to check their communication by comparing Parts A and B.

Tell Me About It (Part A)

Study the picture. Then, ask your partner the questions below. Using your partner's answers, write each underlined name in the correct place on the picture.

Where is the groundskeeper?
Where is the housekeeper?
Where is the hostess?
Where is the waitress?

Where is the bellhop?
Where is the receptionist?
Where is the cashier?
Where is the secretary?

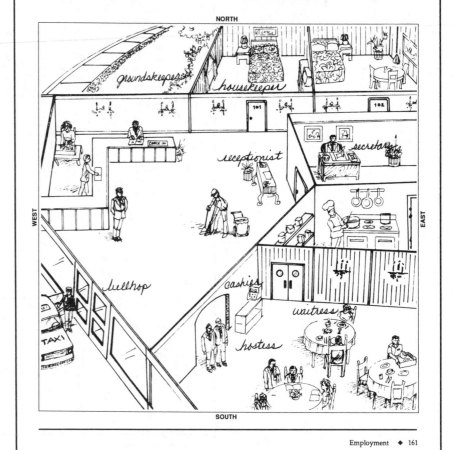

Tell Me About It (Part B)

Study the picture. Then, ask your partner the questions below. Using your partner's answers, write the name of each underlined item in the correct place on the picture.

Where is the <u>cook</u>?
Where is the <u>busboy</u>?
Where is the <u>security guard</u>?
Where is the <u>desk clerk</u>?

Where is the <u>manager</u>?
Where is the <u>custodian</u>?
Where is the <u>operator</u>?
Where is the <u>taxi driver</u>?

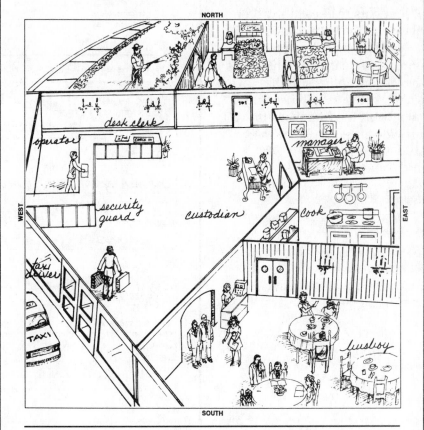

Guess Who, Where, or What

This is a category exercise that can be used with pairs of students in multilevel classes. It can also be completed by individual students. Having students list words under appropriate categories checks their understanding of word meanings.

Students read each word or phrase in the list and decide if it describes a person, place, or thing. Then each student writes the word or phrase in the correct category. You should categorize the first word to provide an example for the students.

Guess Who, Where, or What

Read each word or phrase in the list below. Ask a classmate if the word or phrase describes a person, place, or thing. Write the words in the correct category.

desk clerk	receptionist	job application
wages	custodian	cashier
benefits	lobby	kitchen
restaurant	housekeeper	groundskeeper
job interview	cook	guest rooms
personnel office	hostess	manager
time card	grounds	bellhop

Workers in a Hotel	Places in a Hotel	Things to Ask About a Job
desk clerk	restaurant	wages
receptionist	personnel office	benefits
custodian	lobby	job interview
housekeeper	grounds	time card
cook	kitchen	job application
hostess	guest rooms	
cashier		
groundskeeper		
manager		
bellhop		

Two Against One

This category exercise checks students' understanding of word meaning and usage.

Explain the concept of a set to the class before beginning the exercise.

Ask students to read the three words in each set and then circle the word that doesn't belong to the set. Check the exercise orally by asking students to explain their choices. More than one answer is acceptable in some exercise sets. The students' explanation of their choices determines acceptable answers.

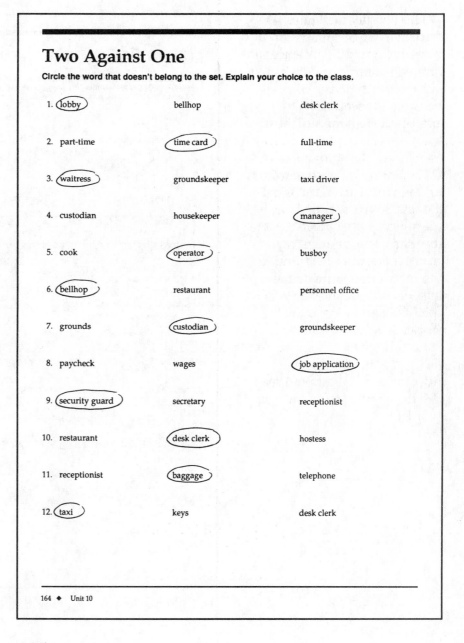

Two Against One

Circle the word that doesn't belong to the set. Explain your choice to the class.

1. (lobby)   bellhop   desk clerk

2. part-time   (time card)   full-time

3. (waitress)   groundskeeper   taxi driver

4. custodian   housekeeper   (manager)

5. cook   (operator)   busboy

6. (bellhop)   restaurant   personnel office

7. grounds   (custodian)   groundskeeper

8. paycheck   wages   (job application)

9. (security guard)   secretary   receptionist

10. restaurant   (desk clerk)   hostess

11. receptionist   (baggage)   telephone

12. (taxi)   keys   desk clerk

Inside Story

This activity facilitates students' use of contextual clues and provides practice in finding synonyms. Rather than just measuring basic comprehension of vocabulary, the exercise fosters the skill of analysis.

First ask the students to read the entire story. Then ask them to find words from the word list that have the same meanings as the words under the blank lines in the story. Instruct the students to write the matching words on the blanks. You may want to fill in the first blank to provide the students with an example. When all the matching words are found and all the blanks are filled in, students should read the story again using the new words.

Inside Story

Read the story below. Choose words or phrases from the list that have the same meanings as the words or phrases under the lines. Write the correct words on the blanks. Read the story again using the words written on the blanks.

part-time	work	paycheck
tired	bellhop	security guard
luggage	afternoon	groundskeeper
cook	time card	Sometimes
morning	Friday	

Sokha the Bellhop

Sokha is a ___*bellhop*___ at the Madison Hotel. He works
       (bag carrier)

___*part-time*___. ___*Sometimes*___ the days seem so long. He
  (half time)   (At times)

punches his ___*time card*___ at 7:30 every ___*morning*___ and
     (time sheet)   (A.M.)

carries ___*luggage*___, opens doors, and answers questions all day.
     (bags)

On Friday he was ___*tired*___. His friend Sam, the
          (sleepy)

___*groundskeeper*___, smiled and gave him a flower. His friend Marcos, the
  (gardener)

___*security guard*___, gave him some coffee. His friend Sally, the
  (night watchman)

___*cook*___, gave him a piece of cake.
  (chef)

Sokha felt better at 3:30 that ___*afternoon*___. Someday he will find better
          (P.M.)

___*work*___. But ___*Friday*___ is pay day, so he picked up
  (employment)   (Fri.)

his ___*paycheck*___ and went to his English class.
   (wages)

Take Your Pick

This multiple choice exercise measures students' understanding of vocabulary meaning and usage in sentences.

Review the unit vocabulary using the pictures at the beginning of the unit. Explain any other new vocabulary in the exercise items before asking students to complete the exercise.

Tell the students to choose the word or phrase missing in each sentence from among the three choices listed under the sentence. Prefixes and suffixes that change word meaning appear in some of the answer choices. Have students write the missing word or phrase on the blank in each sentence.

Take Your Pick

There is a missing word or phrase in each sentence below. Read each sentence. Then, look at the three choices under the sentence. Choose the correct word or phrase and write it on the blank.

1. Urick wanted to _*apply*_ for a job at the hotel.
   apply   application   applying

2. He had to _*fill out*_ an application.
   fill in   fill out   fill about

3. The secretary works forty hours a week. She is a _*full-time*_ employee.
   fill-time   time-full   full-time

4. Raul has _*experience*_ as a security guard.
   experience   experienced   experiencing

5. The custodian _*works*_ from 7:00 A.M. to 3:00 P.M.
   working   works   work

6. The waitress is paid _*by the hour*_ .
   by the hour   by hour   the by hour

7. Erin has an _*interview*_ in thirty minutes.
   interviewing   interviewer   interview

8. Raul read the _*want ads*_ in the Sunday newspaper.
   wanted ads   want ads   ads want

9. Where's the _*personnel office*_ ?
   office personnel   personal office   personnel office

10. There are no _*benefits*_ with this part-time job.
    benefits   benefiting   beneficial

Bingo

1. Make the bingo cards.

Students create bingo cards through teacher dictation of vocabulary. The dictation provides a spelling assessment as well as a listening activity.

Instruct the students to look at the empty bingo grid in their book. The grid has nine squares for nine vocabulary items. Read the vocabulary to the class. Ask students to write the words in the boxes at random, not in rows. Each student should have a different bingo card after nine items are dictated.

2. Check students' spelling.

When the bingo cards are completed, write the vocabulary words on the board and ask students to check their spelling and make corrections.

3. Play bingo.

Distribute eight markers — such as paper clips, buttons, chips, or pennies — to each student. Read each oral cue twice in normal speech. Students find the corresponding vocabulary item on their cards and cover it with a marker. When one student has three in a row, he or she calls "bingo" and then reads off the words in the marked squares for checking. You may need to demonstrate how bingo is played for those students who have never played before.

There are two game options. Choose the one that best fits the students' level of proficiency, or use them both at different times of instruction.

Game 1

Vocabulary for Dictation	Teacher Cues
job	Employment or work.
full-time	Forty hours per week.
part-time	Fewer than forty hours per week.
wages	Money for working.
benefits	Vacation, sick leave, insurance.
job application	Fill this out to get a job.
paycheck	Cash this to get wages.
time card	Shows hours worked.
job interview	Questions and answers about the job.

Game 2

Vocabulary for Dictation	Teacher Cues
housekeeper	Cleans the guest rooms.
desk clerk	Gives out keys to guest rooms.
bellhop	Carries luggage.
security guard	Night watchman.
operator	Answers the phone.
cook	Prepares meals.
manager	Supervises the hotel workers.
taxi driver	Picks up hotel guests at the door.
groundskeeper	Plants flowers and waters the lawn.

Get It Together

The crossword puzzle provides practice in recognizing word meaning and usage.

Have students read each numbered clue and write the answer in the puzzle spaces with the same number. A word list of answers is given so that spelling will not hinder students' ability to complete the puzzle.

To quiz the spelling skills of more advanced students, ask the students to cover the word list while filling in the puzzle squares.

Get It Together

There is a word missing in each sentence below. Choose the correct word from the word list. Print that word in the boxes of the puzzle.

bellhop	taxi	housekeeper	groundskeeper
ads	check	waiter	pay
clerk	full	security	time
hostess			

Across

4. The _____ cleans guest rooms.

6. Look in the want _____ for a job.

8. The desk _____ gives the guest a key to his room.

10. The _____ driver stopped in front of the hotel.

11. The _____ carries your luggage.

Down

1. The _____ plants flowers.

2. Fill out a _____ card.

3. The _____ guard watches over the hotel.

4. The _____ seats people in the restaurant.

5. Pick up your _____ check on Friday.

7. The _____ serves food in the restaurant.

8. Cash your pay _____ .

9. I am looking for _____-time work.

And There's More

1. Charades

Write each job listed below on a 3" x 5" card.

desk clerk	manager
custodian	taxi driver
housekeeper	receptionist
groundskeeper	operator
secretary	waitress
waiter	cook
bellhop	busboy
security guard	

Have one student give non-verbal clues to the class. The student chooses one of the cards and mimes the job duties. The other students try to guess the job title. For example, a student can act out the job duties of a security guard by pretending to use a flashlight to search around a building.

When the job title is guessed, another student chooses a card and continues the game. The game continues until all the cards have been chosen.

2. The Perfect Job

Ask the students to write a description of the perfect job. The description can be imaginative, and the circumstances need not be real. Have the students include the following in their description:

type of work	the job interview
work hours	experience needed
benefits	the job application